TABLE OF CONTENTS

PART 1

Introduction...1
   Disclaimer..4

Why Micropubs..6
   The Companies..6
   Solution..9
   Pub Types...10
   Bermondsey Beer Mile..........................15
   Pro and Cons..17
   The Effects..19
   Measuring Volume................................22

Micropubs..23
   The Burcher's Arms...............................23
   Water Works..28
   Margate and Surrounds........................34
   Little Swift...34
   Fez..36
   The Wheel Ale House............................39
   The Bouncing Barrel..............................40
   The pub Herne Bay................................42
   The Pub Ramsgate.................................43
   The Hovelling Boat Inn..........................44

The Just Reproach..45

Wilds of Surrey Calls..............................47

Real Ale Way 47

Radius Arms 50

Cobbetts 52

The Engine Room.....................................55

The West 59

The Dog House Weymouth 60

The All Hail Ale and The Porterhouse..61

Art Brew 63

The Tap House 67

Cider Barn 69

Brewing Co 70

The Folk Scene...72

First In Last Out 72

Jolly Fisherman 73

Smuggler's Beer and Music 75

Mind The Gap 77

Magnet 78

The Chapel 79

Royston's 79

And There's More 81

The Larkin's Alehouse..........................81

The Dog House Croydon......................85

Worthing 87

Chichester......................................88

The Rake...89

Hoppy Place 89

River Ale House................................91

Four Candles....................................92

Northward Ho!...................................94

The Rusty Barrel 94

The Shambles....................................95

Old Street Tavern and The Blood Bay.98

Stratford Ale House 100

Tamworth Brewing Co 100

Traditional Pubs 101

The Hope 101

The Trafalgar 106

The Sultan 110

Kraft Pub and Kitchen 113

Bricklayers 114

Oaka 117

Chequers 119

King Arthur 120
George and the Dragon 122

Mini Beer Tour 124

PART 2

The Barroom Barrister 134

Introduction 134

A Foetid Stench 144

The Scenario 149

Europe 162

Brexit 171

Drugs 191

Pharma 191
Narcotics 195
Cannabis 200
Cannabis Factories 204

Wokism 209

Entertainment Industry 214
Cancel Culture..................................... 217
Dancing 221

Misogyny 227

Language ....,231

Culture 241

Cultural Appropriation 234

Shariya Law 251

Multi Culturalism 253

Solution 257

The Not-So-Big C 259

PPE 267

Measures 271

The Environment 278

Farming 279

Pollution 285

The Generation Game 291

Shadowy Figures 295

Conclusion..310

PART 1

MY WORLD OF MICROPUB

Introduction

I would like to take you on a tour of the beer scene – and more specifically, the real ale scene – of Great Britain. This should take us on a journey through microbreweries, micropubs and a small number of traditional pubs. Not every micropub, that would be insane. Micros are opening and closing all the time and I'd never be able to keep up. I am, however, a sucker for a micropub and will go in one whenever I am passing one, as long as I have the time and opportunity to do so.

This tome is in two parts, the second part being about the conversations I have had, or at least the subject matters that come up in the course of pub conversation. It is a rant. It is not a transcript of conversations, more an amalgamation of lots of conversations boiled down to its main points.

I will start by giving some of my credentials. Why is it that I believe I have the knowledge to provide this sort of information? Well, let me see. . . I drink beer. That's about all you need to know. As a beer drinker, I like choice, and micropubs and microbreweries offer that. I am a retired police officer who had a job that was mentally very demanding. I was dealing with the seedier side of life – even compared with all the other roles within the job. I needed an outlet. I seldom spoke to my wife about what happened at work because I felt it important to separate the sort of stuff that I was dealing with from my private life. I deliberately sought friends that had nothing to do with my job and I went to places that had no links to people with whom I worked. Even my pastimes were everything my job was not. I play music, I am an artist, I used to build large-scale model tall ships from wood, I cook and I go to pubs.

I know an unhealthy number of brewers who own their own commercial breweries so I get to not only know what is good, but why it is good. I get to sample the highest quality beers made by people who have a passion for it and who do not have accountants watering down their product – metaphorically speaking, of course. I am also getting to know quite a few micropub owners. I own a motorhome and go on trips that seek out different venues to check out their wares. It was probably my good friend Toby, who, when he became a commercial brewer, started talking about micropubs and got me interested.

What I seek to do is to take you through some of my experiences of the micropub world. This is not a reference book to find the best and worst. That is not my intention. Pubs and beer and what we like and dislike are all far too subjective to do that argument any justice. The Campaign for Real Ale (CAMRA) has been trying, and to a large extent, failing to do this for years. When they first started, it was in an era that saw lager and low-quality kegged ale coming more and more to prominence. It wasn't good lager, just alcoholic fizz. Those that still wanted traditional English-style ale were struggling to find much out there. They started their campaign with a view to bringing ale back into prominence. They started judging beer to encourage brewers to improve their product. They insisted that any beer that had the word 'real' attached to it must have only natural ingredients. They produced a guidebook of pubs that sold real ale to a consistent standard to encourage the retail of the finest quality. By and large, after something in the order of 50 years, they succeeded in their endeavours and we now have pubs vying to be included in their annual beer guide. It is, after all, free advertising. Because CAMRA has succeeded, they need to maintain a holding pattern so that the standards don't start to slip. The problem is that their raison d'êtrer has gone. They have succeeded. Some feel that their relevance has gone with it. They need to try to make themselves relevant again.

One of their ideas is the 'champion beers of Great Britain', which seeks out the best beer in the country every year. But how do you do that? There are so many different styles of beer and so many different taste buds out there. How can one compare completely different beers such as a bitter, an Australian hopped pale and a stout? It is like comparing apples and pears, subjective and pointless. There is no comparison, so leave it. It isn't just that, it is also the fact that different people like different tastes, so one may well believe that what they are tasting is the finest thing the world has ever produced, but the guy sitting next to him may think it undrinkable slop. Neither are wrong. They do have categories, which is more sensible, but they need to leave it there. Because they don't, the choices for the accolade of best beer of Great Britain all seem to be the least offensive or the most average beer. What they consider very good is often nowhere near what I think of as good. I want powerfully hopped light beers using new world hops or dark and gloopy stouts. Everything else, to me, is dull and uninteresting. CAMRA tend to go for middle-of-the-road low 'alcohol by volume' (ABV) beers that leave an acrid aftertaste from the locally produced earthy hops for which England is famous. Not my mug of beer. CAMRA seems slightly better at identifying good pubs, but I have issues too many to go into here, about how they deal with this selection process.

Disclaimer

The reader may feel that some of the statements made hereinafter are quite sweeping and don't hold up to scrutiny. Please note that this is all my opinion and not necessarily widely held. I will use the word 'most' rather than 'all' to soften the message without watering down my opinion. For all the bad pubs, bad beers, bad publicans and bad freeholders, there are good ones out there as well. Where compliments are due, I will name the subject where I can and will avoid identifying by name, the bad ones. People never mind a compliment but will challenge a bad comment, even if it is an opinion and especially if it is true.

I would also like to apologise in advance if I appear to be 'mansplaining' certain phrases. I have a connection with people outside the UK and some of the sort of language used by beery people, and their practises will not be familiar to those people. There also may be people out there who don't know some things that come naturally to others, so I have to give a nod to them and not confuse matters. I will keep explanations brief

So, welcome to my world of beer and micropubs. Please go into them wherever you find them. They are interesting places.

Why Micropub?

Why Micropub? What is wrong with the good, old-fashioned traditional British pub? It has served us well for hundreds of years. What has changed?

<u>The companies</u>

Most of the traditional pubs are either owned by organisations that are known as Pub Cos or they are owned by major breweries. Many of the major breweries and pubcos operate in a similar way to each other. They seem to be mercenary and their practices stifle the pub trade. Consider this. If a brewery owns a pub (known as a 'tied' pub as the licensee is tied to a contract that ensures they source their product from the company), they don't have any middlemen to deal with, they just have to supply the pub, at cost, and take the profit from the sale. Too easy, it seems. What they do, is lease the pub to a person who will run it as their own company. The terms of the lease state that the licensee source all their product through the brewery. The brewery then sells its own product, to its own pubs, often at inflated prices so the publican can't make a decent living. This is why, if you go into a tied brewery-owned pub, the beer is so expensive. It is not the guy running the place, it is the brewery.

Free houses are those that are supposedly free of tie but many are owned by companies that are either a pubco or act in the same way as pub cos, so not really free of the umbrella company. The company may be able to source products from wherever they want to but the guy running the pub, with what one would hope is a decent knowledge of what his customers want, cannot.

Pub Cos are companies that specialise in owning real estate. They own a lot of pubs. I'm sure that some of these companies are decent. I haven't heard of one yet, but they must be out there somewhere. The way they operate, it seems to me, is that they obtain the freehold on a pub and sell the leasehold to people who want to run them. This all seems quite straightforward. The problem comes in the contracts these companies are offering. One has to buy the leasehold from them. They will sell this on the understanding that the prospective publicans will pay a ground rent that is set by the company and can be increased at their pleasure after set periods. The leaseholders will be contractually obliged to source all their products through the company. A bit harsh, but we can live with that, can't we? Because you are contracted to buy everything from them, they can charge what they want. Most seem to stock the cheapest product on the market, then sell it to the pub at a price that means the licensee cannot take any real profit. Because the company can also up the ground rent to whatever they want, they keep an eye on how the pub is doing, and when they see that it is becoming successful, they slap on an increase at the following rent review. If the pub isn't doing that well and they can't justify upping the rent, they will often persuade the incumbents to move on so that they can get a new licensee and charge them more. Rather than allowing the publican to make a little money out of success, they want to take everything they can. In so doing, it is almost impossible to make any money from owning one of these pubs. All the while, the publican is self-employed, so the company don't have to worry about the wages of the publican or the staff, and they insist that any issues with the building and contents are dealt with by the publican. The publican is the licensee and has to abide by the conditions of the licence set by the licensing authority. The freeholders have no such issues, the authority will look to the licensee if there are any problems with the premises. So the ground rent pays for nothing other than the right to trade from that premises. On top of all this, they seem to treat their publicans and their suppliers with disdain. These companies insist on payment by the tenant straight away but many fail to pay their own suppliers on time.

So, we have a brewery industry that is so focused on making a profit for itself that it does not care about the customer. They are controlled by moneymen who insist on spending as little as possible on ingredients. This means that the beer produced by most major breweries is low quality and, because of their huge overheads, their prices are over the top. We also have a pubco industry whose only thought is to have as much income as possible for as little expenditure as they can get away with, publicans and pubgoers be damned. Life would be so much easier if they didn't have to rely on the public to buy the stuff.

The solution

There are, despite all this, still plenty of people out there who want to run a pub. The way around all this trouble is to utilise the relatively recently relaxed licensing rules. Find a small shop front that has no links to the pub or brewing industry, tart it up and get a licence to sell beer for consumption on the premises. There are so many micro and mini breweries around that they have no issues around sourcing decent beer without going through major breweries. So, no pub cos, no major breweries, no limitations on who you source from. The person has the freedom – within the conditions of the rental agreement and the licencing conditions – to do whatever that person wants to attract customers. What you then get is establishments that can cater for whatever demographic they want. They can let their customers guide them in the type of product they sell. There are comparatively low overheads, and the product is sourced from breweries in a free market environment. This means that the prices at the pump are much lower. The premises are normally too small to have pool tables or dartboards. Music is generally kept low or off completely. Some even encourage live music. This is dependent on the licencing conditions and what the customers want. That is the difference between micropubs and their big brothers. You either know what you want in a pub and go to whichever pub caters for that taste, or you become a regular at a micro pub and help shape how it continues.

Pub types

It feels to me that there are two main types of micropub and several sub-categories. The hipster pub that serves beer from a keg or 'key-keg' and those that have cask ales as their main product with some kegged beer and cider are the main two. The hipster pubs are often extortionately expensive. They tend to serve beer in two-third-pint glasses and charge for what I would consider an expensive full pint. I am told that the kegs that they use in key-keg beers are single-use plastics, so they have to use new kegs every time they brew. Those costs are passed onto the customer, so we are paying for a fresh keg for every 40 litres brewed. I also find these places a little staid. They have sharp bar staff in sharp clothing and sharply styled facial hair. They have smartly painted grey interiors, swish furnishings which are all hard metal and plastic and have no character whatsoever. As there is no soft furnishing, if you get more than three people talking at the same time, it's a cacophony because everything echoes. You can't hold a conversation with anyone without having to shout even louder than everyone else. I like a chat, so these places are not really for me. I will go into them to try them out, but I won't pay £8-a-pint when I can get the highest quality beer for a little over half that price.

Here is where I start with my issues over semantics when it comes to beer. It seems that the trend is towards calling any kind of kegged beer that isn't massed-produced rubbish, 'Craft beer', thereby differentiating it from cask ale. I would suggest that as much if not more craft goes into producing and keeping cask ales than the fizz that comes out of the keg. It is brewed in the same way, has a similar fomentation period and similar ingredients. The only difference is that lager should be conditioned at a colder temperature over a longer period. This time spent conditioning would normally have the effect of causing mild effervescence and a more developed flavour, but I don't believe this happens anymore, the brewers just introduce CO2 at the pump thereby doing away with the need to condition their product any more than cask beers. So the word 'craft' is, in my opinion, being misused. And the extra price tag, which tends to be at least 25 per cent more, is unjustified. I think that people believe that if you put the word 'craft' or 'artisan' in the name of their product, they can automatically up the price. Unfortunately, the paying public appears to agree. This was demonstrated to me recently when a local brewery who tend to specialise in the kegged beers, produced a cask ale. I believe that they used a recipe from one of their kegged beers and conditioned it in a cask. This sounds fine but the problems come when you get away with a lack of flavour by serving it cold and fizzy then use the same beer – same ingredients, same brewing time- only served at room temperature without the excessive fizz. This beer, which was 5.2 abv, so not weak, was bereft of anything approximating taste. This can only be due to a lack of ingredients. You can't hide your lack of 'craft' behind cold temperatures and fizz in cask ale.

The one other thing that 'craft' beer producers haven't got through their skulls is that dark beers are best served a few degrees below room temperature, not three degrees Celsius. Scientists will tell you that our taste buds start becoming ineffective below eight degrees and are more or less useless below three degrees. Why would anyone spend time, energy and money creating something with so many complex taste notes, only to freeze everyone's taste buds as they drink the stuff? Makes no sense. Brew it cold if you must but serve it just below room temperature.

The other pub type – the type of place I tend to frequent – seems to be able to keep their prices competitive and their décor is designed for comfort. They rely largely on cask-conditioned beer. It is unpasteurised and therefore needs to be looked after. Once it is open it has to be used within days and so they need customers that want to drink the stuff. It is normally served a few degrees below room temperature, so they can't hide from poor quality and bad-tasting beer. These are places you go to have a beer and a chat. The demographic is slightly older than your average hipster. Some tend to be so small that everyone in the pub is engaged in the same conversations. Strangers and regulars alike. The hipster pub is a place to meet people you know and go on from there to a restaurant or club. The micro is a place to meet people, be it people who go there regularly or those who are just passing. It is easy to strike up a conversation with anyone. It is not considered weird or needy to start chatting with someone sitting next to you. Nor is it a problem to sit at a table at which other people are seated. Obviously, one has to observe the niceties by making sure you aren't plonking yourself down in a seat that someone else is using, but it is perfectly acceptable and encouraged in many of these places. These pubs are not normally used as a staging post to launch an evening of drink and debauchery at the local nightclub so one would probably either go there for one or two then go home or make an evening of it and stay there until it closes.

I imagine many youngsters would not understand my type of pub in the same way as I don't understand their hipster pubs. Life would be dull if we all liked the same things.

There is a third type that is laughably called a 'sports bar' which just means a bunch of out-of-condition, middle-aged and older blokes sitting in a pub drinking low-quality lager and watching football. The idea that any of them have ever been actual sportsmen is obviously never in the mix. And there is only one sport – football. Occasionally one may find a dartboard so the real sporty people can work up an adrenalin rush prior to watching football. The premises are often small and have more TV screens than the wall space allows. There is one such place in East Grinstead. There is seating for about 12 people in a room the size of a small living room and two huge TV screens both mercifully showing the same game. I am taking it that the customers do not want to expend energy turning their heads through 90 degrees in order to watch this stuff, so they arrange it so that customer movement is kept to an absolute minimum. Nor do they want to hassle with choosing what beer they want. Any old rubbish that comes out of the pump will do.

Running alongside this there is another category, and pubs can be categorised in three different ways. You have the local's pub, the pub that relies on passing trade and the type that sits somewhere in the middle. The hipster pubs tend to be on or near high streets and train stations and rely on passing trade almost exclusively. My type of pub tends to be a little more varied. Some are almost exclusively for locals and the odd waif or stray that wonders in there as a result of what someone may have said by way of recommendation. Many are on or near the high street but always seem to have a hard core of regulars that keep the till ticking over while they are waiting to ensnare an innocent passer-by to partake in their offerings

In addition to this, we also have your Microbrewery, many of which have their own tap rooms which often have all the same attributes as a micropub. If they specialise in kegged beer, it will be the expensive hipster-type pub. This really winds me up. No middlemen and low overheads and yet they are often more expensive than the pubs they supply. If they specialise in cask beers then they are more akin to the micropubs I frequent.

The Bermondsey Beer Mile

For those whose topographic knowledge of London is lacking, Bermondsey is an area on the South bank of the Thames on the other side of the river to the City of London and Whitechapel (of Jack the Ripper fame). The entire area was lawless marshlands in Tudor times with the only access being via London Bridge. It was only when Marc Isambard Brunel, father of Isambard Kingdom Brunel and all that followed, managed to work out how to build on the land that the whole area all the way to Wimbledon Common started to be tamed in Victorian times. The foundations of all the buildings had to be very robust to prevent them from sinking into the mud. In modern-day Bermondsey in South London, there is an overground train track that leads into London Bridge train station from the east. It is kept away from the traffic on raised railway lines. Below the lines are arches, and these arches, which are as tall as a two-storey building less the roof, are now used for small retail shops. They were once dead spaces owned by the railway and have, over the years, been occupied by various shops. There were five breweries at various points along this track the last time I walked it. They are all hipster breweries that have small areas set aside for consumption on the premises. So these places do not even have to transport their beer. It is already on site. They still manage to charge 30% more for a pint of beer than the surrounding pubs. The beer is normally decent quality – although not 30% better than the other pubs. As the name suggests, it is about a mile from start to finish. The first time I walked this when we had come to the end and it was time to go, we simply carried on in the direction we were going heading for London Bridge station. A few hundred yards into the journey, we came across another pub/brewery. A sixth one that was not advertised as part of the beer mile. (Maybe they just didn't want to call it the beer mile-and-two-hundred-yards, I don't know) This one, however, was not hipster, they produced cask ales at slightly less than local pub prices. The beer was fine, nothing remarkable, but perfectly quaffable. So now when I go to Bermondsey, I skip the first five and just go straight in there. It's easy to get to, unpretentious and inexpensive.

Micropubs tick many of the boxes I like to see ticked. There are downsides, but nothing that can't be dealt with. Those of us who prefer a fizzy alcoholic beverage that does little more than intoxicate and has no real taste are fine – they can go to any pub in the country and find what they want. Many of my contemporaries and I, steer away from fizz pop as I like to refer to it – without substance, tasteless, alcoholic fizz – for something with more taste. I don't tend to drink alcohol in order to get drunk. I do get drunk sometimes, but I can also have two or three and go home happy. Beer is therefore not used to drown sorrows or forget for a moment, the mess we have created in the world. It is a social lubricant that, used sensibly is exactly what we need.

Whenever I go into a pub that is not serving the sort of beer I want, I turn around and walk out. It is often not the fault of the publican, just the fact that the beer is not what I want and I see no reason to pay good money to buy something I don't want. I wouldn't go into a clothes shop and buy a pair of trousers that I don't like so why would I go into a pub and buy beer I don't like? I am aware that many people do, but not me.

Pros and cons

I suppose the problems and the advantages are along the same lines as each other:

- On the good side, most have an ever-changing selection of beers. This means that there is always something new to try out. If the publican is serving the sort of stuff that I like, this is normally good.

- On the negative side, most have an ever-changing selection of beers which means that if I have found one that I like, there is a probability that the barrel will come to an end and a different one will take its place. The replacement may, or may not, be to my taste.

- On the good side, they are often small, intimate places where you can interact with everyone.

- On the bad side, they are sometimes small and intimate and it is therefore difficult to avoid people who you wish to avoid.

- On the positive side, the beer is almost invariably good quality well-kept beer by someone who cares about his product.

- On the negative side, I am only exposed to good quality beer, anything less won't do. I become fussy about what I drink and where I drink. I become a beer snob.

The main point is that they are all different and the publicans are out to please their customers, unlike the larger pub who basically say, 'If you don't like it, there are plenty of other pubs around.'

The effects

To me, it is all very positive because the little guy is sticking it to the big guys for once. Look at the high street in England today. For me, the best towns to visit are those that don't have big multicorporate chain stores clogging up the high street. Places like Rye in Sussex, Malden, Essex and Totnes in Devon are nice places to go because the high street has interesting stuff being sold by small independent traders. Most high streets in most towns do not have a pet shop anymore, because big corporate warehouses have put them all out of business. Try to find an independent menswear shop in Reading. You'll struggle and end up going into one of the chain stores that have three storeys of womenswear an entire floor devoted to kids and one aisle at the back of the shop that has two jeans, two types of other trousers, two t-shirts, two collared shirts and two suits (one black and one grey). This is because the little guy has been overwhelmed by multi-corporates. I believe a town isn't a town unless it has a proper pet shop, a proper hardware shop that is slightly chaotic but the owner knows where everything is and he has everything. Slightly chaotic bicycle shops are the same. Again, they have all been put out of business by huge DIY chains.

The thing is, that all these places started as small independents and have succumbed to big business. The pub scene of the last century or so is different. All the pubs were owned by the big guys. They decided what you drank and where you drank it. If a small independent started getting successful and having ideas above their station, the local major brewer would step in, buy it out, often at above the going rate, and close it down.

'We can't have young up-starts giving people choice! Where will it all end?'

For years we have been fed on beer that didn't really differ from one brewery to the next, both in price and flavour. They had their own different styles of beer. But they all had roughly the same range. A weak brown ale bitter; a stronger brown ale; a weak IPA that wasn't really an IPA but rather a slightly lighter coloured bitter; a strong IPA; some sort of dark porter or stout that would only come out in the winter. There are many more styles of beers out there, but this is what you were offered in most pubs at the time if you were lucky – most would only offer a bitter and in IPA and nothing else. The micropub industry has put the cat among the pigeons here and is taking business away from the big guys. Not so as to seriously damage their business models, but enough to make them think.

It appears to have come from the financial crisis around the turn of the 21st century, where many wealthy bankers and financiers were finding themselves unemployed and so thought to themselves, 'I drink beer, I have knocked out the odd home-brew that didn't hospitalise anyone permanently. I have a few quid burning a hole in my pocket. Why shouldn't I make beer myself on a larger scale? What could possibly go wrong? The better ones went on to become very successful. Most faded and died. But on the back of this, with the high street pubs struggling under the yoke of the multi-corporates screwing them for everything they owned, the micropub emerged to complement the micro-brewery. These small independent breweries were innovating and changing ideas on what 'flavour balance' was all about. The idea that if you wanted flavour, you had to have a strong beer was thrown out of the window. One of the first successful micro-breweries was Dark Star. It began life in a small pub in Brighton. It was run by three youngish blokes with a taste for the music of the Grateful Dead (Hence 'Dark Star'). They produced, as their signature beer, a low ABV beer that was full of flavour by using new-world hops to give an aromatic citrus flavour. This beer fairly marched out of the pumps and everyone else cottoned on. Because the micro-pubs were not restricted in terms of where they sourced from, they could put these beers in their pubs. As the micropub industry has grown, the microbrewery industry has followed. Some of the major breweries have experimented with these ideas but the moneymen will always make sure they don't use enough ingredients and therefore produce something that is not quite up to scratch. Just the fact they are doing this shows the impact the little guy is making and this pleases me. There are still plenty of people out there who are happy with the beer that major brewers produce. That is great, something for everyone at last.

Measuring volume

One more thing to cover before moving on to the pubs and I apologise in advance for being boring (if it's not too late). It is just easier to clarify here. I will be referring to the size of breweries using an industry standard, the Barrel. A barrel is a specific measurement which works out as a smidgen under 35 gallons. A 'ten-barrel brewery' is considered a microbrewery. Major breweries go into the hundreds and even thousands but there are one-barrel breweries around as well as everything in between. When we look at casks, they normally come in 36 pint pins, 9-gallon or 18-gallon cask sizes and microbreweries normally stick with the smaller ones. This all means that a ten-barrel brewery can produce a little under 40 9-gallon casks per brew at any given time.

Micropubs

The Butchers Arms

Here is where I take you on a journey of the pubs I have visited. This will be in no particular order on any measurement, although I will start with the one that claims to be the first in the UK.

The Butcher's Arms. Herne Village, Kent

Something I should mention is that the prefix 'micro' does not necessarily refer to the size of the pub. There are some relatively large micropubs around. The one thing they all have in common is that the premises does not have a pub history. This was made clear by the good-natured argument that occurred between the one that the owners claim to be the first micropub in the country, the Butchers Arms, Herne Village, Kent, and the Nutshell pub in Bury St

Edmunds, Suffolk. For many years, the Nutshell claimed to be the smallest pub in Britain and was actually named as such in the Guinness Book of Records. Despite evidence to the contrary, they still hold this claim on their web page. It could remain accurate if they prefixed 'pub' with 'Traditional'. They were never a micro, as the premises has been a pub for 155 years. They claimed to have managed to squeeze in 102 people, but there was no room to move, so it was a pointless exercise outside the purely academic. It is generally said that it can serve one rugby side, that is fifteen men at any one time. It was tiny. It is a tied pub owned by Greene King, a brewery that specialises in producing dull, uninteresting, tasteless beer (my opinion). The Butcher's Arms started life as a butcher shop. This is an ideal premises as it came with a cold room, perfect for the much-needed temperature-controlled atmosphere that real ale needs. Inside, the tables you place your beer on are used butcher's blocks, so there are no flat surfaces. There is seating room for nine people at a squeeze and standing room for a further three or four. Very small.

The two pubs each claimed to be the smallest. An argument that should be easy to resolve. Measure it and see how many people fit in there. That didn't happen because the Nutshell would have lost their claim. I suppose they just decided that the Butcher's Arms wasn't a proper pub, so there was no argument. The Nutshell then opened the upstairs for customers, increasing the floor space substantially, making the Butchers Arms not only the first Micro but the undisputed smallest at the time. With the proliferation of the micropub industry, this is now all academic, and there are probably a dozen similar-sized pubs around.

So, the Butchers was the first micropub that I went to. Herne Village is a very small village on the other side of the main road linking all the towns along the southern bank of the Thames inlet. Herne Bay being the nearest large town. The village had one convenience store, three pubs and a few houses. The pub is run by a one-armed man called Martin and his mate, whose name escapes me. He has all his beers on stillage (this means that all the beer was poured direct from the cask, so there is no need to keep lines clean and maintain handpumps. Stillage refers to the frame in which the barrels are held). These he kept in the built-in cold room behind the main pub that customers had to walk through to get to the toilet. He had a system installed that meant he could put the casks into the stillage, then spile and tap them without anyone else getting involved. He had six beers on at any one time and another six ready for when the next one went off. They were all real ale, ranged between 3.6% abv to 7+%, and were either bitter, pale ale, or IPA in style. He had a few wines and spirits but only a few. He was – and probably still is – a taciturn chap at the best of times, but this just added to the charm of the place. There were no private conversations as it was too small, so as you entered the pub, you were immediately drawn into whatever conversation was happening at the time. The décor was an odd assortment of toys and skeletons hanging from the ceiling for no reason other than the fact that a customer put it there.

Because Martin only has one arm, he made it plain that he preferred it, that if you were ordering two pints, they would be the same so that he could pour it straight into a two-pint jug and hand us two empty glasses for us to do the honours. It wasn't a hard and fast rule; it just made his life easier. He also only collected payment at the end of the evening rather than after each order. It always felt a little odd to me. Very European in a very English setting. He knew his customers and they knew him. It has been a few years since I have been back. What with lockdown and new pubs opening all the time and his erratic opening times, I have not had the opportunity. It was, however, a great little place. I never witnessed any trouble. Lager louts would never bother us. In fact, you had to look out for the pub if you were going there. If you did not know of the place, you could probably walk past it every day and not know it was there. This was deliberate because he was only interested in his demographic and was happy to continue that way. There are plenty of pubs for trouble seekers and louts; they don't need to bother us.

Because this pub is 80 miles from where we live, we used to book into a campsite about two miles from the pub and use that as a base. Over the years, other people came with us, and we brought business their way. Not much, but not nothing, either. We always camped in the quietest corner so that we wouldn't be bothered by kids playing at ungodly hours of the morning. One day we had to take our dog with us. As they do not accept pets on the premises, we left the dog with my sister, who lived pretty nearby. Poor old Tike, who was a soft creature, howled from the moment we went to the moment we returned the following day, leaving the entire household, if not the whole street, without sleep. A second night there was out of the question. We went to the owners to see if there was any leeway, but they wouldn't entertain it. I have no problem with this. That is their policy, which is fine, but we couldn't stay there. They made it plain to us that we wouldn't get our money back. We said that some friends were coming to stay that evening and could they use that space as it was already paid for and would be unused. No, they would have to pay. Our site was ours; if we chose not to stay there, that was our choice. Basically, the people were unnecessarily unfriendly to the point of nasty and had clearly decided they didn't want our business or any of the business we brought them. We left there and have never returned and always told anyone who would go there of this story.

About a mile from the site was a small brewery, Goody Ales, on a large piece of land with its own brewery tap. The brewery was not really to my taste, but we went there to reset and figure out what to do. We got chatting to the staff and asked about their neighbours. When they heard the story, they told us to pitch up in their extensive backyard for no charge as long as we were using their pub. So this is what we did. It was a good evening. The beer was not great, but the evening was good, and we left there with a good feeling.

We found out the following year that the campsite got wind of the fact that the brewery was allowing people to stay and put in a complaint, meaning that the brewery can no longer allow camping on the brewery grounds. So now we can't use that brewery either. We have nowhere to stay if we want to visit the Butcher's Arms, so we can't go there, and we certainly would not go to the campsite for all the tea in China. They have taken business away from themselves and two other companies just because they could. Oh, and the name? Bragg Lane Farm Campsite. Won't see you there. . . ever. ☐

The Water Works

Where to next? Rye. While I re-assert that this is not a guide, nor is it in any order, this is one of my favourites. It not only ticks all the boxes, but the publican has also invented more boxes to tick. . . and then ticked them.

The Water Works Micro, Rye East Sussex

In a town steeped in history, this micropub has a history all of its own. When you go in there, you will see a timeline of the building's various uses through the centuries. The town is close to Pevensey, the place where the Normans landed in 1066 in the last successful military invasion of the island, so it has plenty of history. Although it is a few miles from the coast, it was, at that time, a coastal port. The build-up of silt in the river has meant that both Pevensey and Rye are no longer seaside towns. Rye prides itself on a town that only welcomes independent traders meaning that there are only two shops in town that are chain stores. Because of this, they are happy to see this type of pub.

The building itself started its life as a waterworks and supplied Rye with fresh water in days of yore. As technology grew, the works stopped being used and has been many different things through the ages, including being a public convenience. Prior to becoming a pub, it was a curio shop, and it continues in this role even today. I believe the pub owner, Dave, gets the premises for a low rent on the understanding that he continues to sell their stuff. As a result, everything in the pub is for sale, including the table at which you may be seated and the chair on which you sit. They all have price tags, and if someone comes in and says, 'I want that table!' Dave will approach whoever is sitting there, ask them to remove all their belongings, remove the table and replace it with a completely different one. All of this, you may feel, would be a real problem, but Dave is so good with people; he makes it easy, and it becomes part of the pub's charm.

The premise of this pub is that it is there to bring the community and its visitors together. There is a sign in the pub saying something to the effect of 'micropubs are for sharing. Come in, plonk yourself down on a vacant seat and talk to the person sitting next to you.' He not only encourages everyone to have a conversation with everyone else, but he also almost enforces it. You walk into the pub and see an empty table; you and your companion sit at the table, ready to go to the bar and order your first drink. Dave will welcome you in and ask that, rather than sitting at opposite ends of the table, you sit next to each other. Then when someone else comes in, they are encouraged to sit at the same table. You invariably start chatting with these strangers and, despite any initial reservations, end up having an interesting time, possibly learning one or two things along the way. I have been there sitting at a table when a small group of people have come in, sat, and chatted for 45 minutes over a pint, then moved on to wherever they were going. Before long, another bunch of people are sitting and chatting, and I have ended up having chats with a dozen different people about everything and nothing all in the same evening. When lock down came along, all pubs were damaged. This one was significantly affected because he couldn't do what he had always done when they eventually reopened, so the conversation dried up. It has all returned to something akin to normal, but it was a long and painful process.

It is also a dog-friendly pub. Dave absolutely dotes on each and every animal that comes into the pub. Being so small, this is not the place to be if you don't like dogs. Not a problem for me; I find it difficult to trust people who don't like animals, so I have little sympathy with those that don't.

As for beer selection, he always has eight ever-changing cask ales on, eight ciders at all times, a couple of kegged beers, plus some good bar snacks. There is also a good gin selection and a selection of wine. I have only seen a television in there once. It was put in there to watch an international sporting contest – not football – and he made amends by going to a local chip shop and ordering chips sufficient for everyone in the pub, all on the house.

As far as décor, it is ever-changing because it's all for sale. You may start off with a large round table that seats six people and end up with a square art deco four-seater. The chairs also change constantly. Many pubs I go into have a seat where one regular always sits. Everyone knows this. It is an unspoken but hard and fast rule, nonetheless. This pub does not have that because the chair is never there long enough.

There are one or two things that make me chuckle when I go there. There is a pump clip for Doombar, a beer that is possibly the dullest, most boring beer in the country. When the brewery unsuccessfully approached Dave to sell their product, they left the pump clip with him. He approached his customers for ideas on what to do with it.

Dave feels the same as I do about Doombar, so, as a result of his straw poll, the pump clip is in the gent's toilet and is the toilet flush. We all know what Doombar tastes like, so a more appropriate place to have it would be hard to find. Another less advisable thing was the name of a beer. They have recently started brewing their own product. The town being Rye and the premises being the site of a public convenience, they seem to believe that a good name for a beer is 'Uryenal'. I will concede that this is clever, but I don't think I want to drink something that is a homophone of urinal. It's not really my kind of beer anyway, so it will never be a problem. If I think this — and I am not squeamish — then there must be others who think the same.

This pub is 50 miles from where I live, so it isn't the place to pop out to for a quick half. We own a motorhome and stay overnight if we go there. Despite this, I have met friends from my local area in there; I have met people who have grown up in my area and know the place well; I have met imternational travellers, local people and visitors of all shapes and sizes, and it seems, have talked to most. It is an excellent little town with an excellent little pub to complement it — as long as you like dogs.

I have been into some pubs once, so I can't give a rounded commentary on them. Around the coast, stretching from

Herne Bay to Deal in Kent, there are many micro pubs opening and closing all the time. Some I go into whenever I am in the area, some we go into to have a look. They are in here, dotted about randomly, because there was something about them that I liked.

Margate and Surrounds

I am not a seaside resort type of person. My brother and sister, however, are. Because of this, I have to go there fairly regularly to help with ongoing family health issues. Never being one to let an opportunity slide, I take the opportunity to visit the many and varied hostelries in the town. If you don't count Westgate and Cliftonville – two of Margate's satellite towns – there are six micropubs. The first one you come to is called Ales of the Unexpected. An excellent name for a pub, although the ales are less than surprising. I went in there one weekend on one of the rare occasions that I was there without my long-suffering wife. Only five or six people were in there and were all near the bar chatting amongst themselves. They welcomed me in there as if I was a regular, plonked me down within their group and carried on chatting. It was a really nice place to be welcomed to. The beer had little in the way of range, all middle-of-the-road light ales and bitters, so not really to my tastes, but I enjoyed it so much that I overlooked that and just drank the least offensive one

Little Swift, Margate, Kent

One of the first ones we ever went into was The Little Swift. This one is a bit hipster for my tastes, but the publican and his partner are very good at what they do, so I can forgive them for that. I say this because of my appreciation for the skills of bar staff. These skills include but are not limited to knowing your customer, remembering what they like and knowing who is next in line. Regular pubgoers will be aware that, although there are no formal queues, they are there. It is the better bar staff members who know who is next. My wife and I went in there for the first time circa 2018. We had a conversation with the guy who runs the place and had a thoroughly pleasant evening. We returned there about four months later, and not only did he remember us, but he also remembered the conversation and what my wife and I were drinking. Given the number of people who will have passed through his doors in four months, I think this was an astonishing feat. Either that or my wife and I are particularly memorable. The former may be more accurate.

The next one along is an old geezers-type pub. All cask ale but little in the way of range or atmosphere, so I don't bother. A couple of doors down is a brewery pub with a small two-barrel brewery on site. Again, this is a little hipster, and given that there are no middlemen, the beer is a little on the expensive side. It's all very sharp, modern, and free of anything that approximates an atmosphere. As one looks out of this pub across the bay. You see a concrete pier extending out, forming an enclosed harbour. Along this pier are several shops, coffee places, and a micropub called the Harbour Arms. It has strange and erratic opening times but, because one can see whether or not it is open from the main road, looking across the harbour, you don't have to waste a journey. This pub boasts a good range of beers and wines, not much in the way of seating inside but plenty outside. Reasonably priced and the sort of place where one will invariably get involved in some sort of conversation.

 Fez, Margate, Kent

All this leads to the pub I always go into whenever I'm in Margate. The Fez. This pub is the very reason why I won't rate these pubs as good, bad or indifferent because this one is definitely not to everyone's taste. The Fez is owned by an ex-arts professor who has used the place as a canvas to express himself. It is quirky. All the seating is entirely disparate. There is a seat by the window that came off a 70s fairground ride, a 1970s hairdresser's seat complete with a hair drier. There is a bus seat with an old pinball table used as a table and theatre seats along the wall where all the locals congregate. There is seating for about 20 people, and every one is different. The walls and ceiling are packed full of quirks and quiddities. It is like one of those highly detailed paintings with many things going on, and you see something different every time you look at it. Every time I go in there, I see something new – even though it has always been there.

There is an area of the ceiling devoted to brass musical instruments and a big sign saying 'Way Out', despite the fact that it is a tiny place and it is obvious where the only door to the place is. I will probably never stop discovering new oddities; there are so many things there. They have a 1960s/1970s feel to it all. Advertising banners, sooty puppets and all manner of things that take me back to my childhood and teen years. Statler and Waldorf, the Muppet show's grumpy old men peer down on the hoy polloi, probably making disparaging comments about all and sundry. It may be small, but they play music that is typically 60s and 70s stuff, and people get up and dance. There is always a conversation to be had. People who are travelling through go in there and mingle with the locals. There is a very specific local group in there whenever I go, and we have come to know each other. I took my guitar in there once, only because I didn't want to leave it in the car. The landlord instructed me to play a tune, so I played the Sound of Silence and received a pint for my pains (or is that the other customers' pain?). The beer range isn't brilliant, but there usually is something I can use, and whenever the landlord is in, he comes over to say hello. I even went there one evening to find myself talking to a couple who recognised us from one of my local establishments (Now sadly closed) in South Wimbledon. We had a long chat about a dozen mutual acquaintances. Bearing in mind that I live 80 miles away, I am treated as a local, and it is a very comfortable feeling.

There are other pubs nearby. The Bake and Ale Micro in Westgate, a mile or so from the outskirts of Margate town centre, was opened twelve years ago. The premises had something to do with the baking industry as, I believe, did the original owner's wife, hence the name. I will go in there occasionally, but it is only open a few hours three days a week, and it has changed owners, so I can make little in the way of informed judgements.

Cliftonville, in the opposite direction to Westgate, boasts a couple of micros. The Bank on the site of a closed down . . . err . . . bank. The beer range is good, but no atmosphere, and it has the distinct disadvantage of being in Cliftonville. The Laughing Barrel we went into as we were coming out of lockdown. It was making a good fist of what they were doing. This is a pub that was built up from the latrines of a previous pub that no longer exists. We quite liked the pub, but it is in Cliftonville. It isn't even a place you'd drive through to go somewhere else; you'd just avoid it and drive around. We don't go in there often.

The Wheel Alehouse, Birchington Kent

Heading west out of Margate, just past Westgate, you find another small seaside resort called Birchington. I would say that this town felt really odd to me because it didn't feel like a seaside town. Directions to the beach seemed somewhat incongruous, yet it is on the sea, with a beach and everything. It has a pleasant mix of big chain supermarkets living cheek-by-jowl with small independent shops. I couldn't understand why one would allow two Co-op Supermarkets and a Sainsbury's all within 100 yards of each other, but if that is what the town planners think is a good thing, then who am I to criticise? There also seemed to be more pet shops, animal rescues, animal charities and vets than you could shake a stick at. All this in a town that you could walk through in ten minutes.

Within this little town was our latest micropub find. The Wheel Alehouse. Not typically my favourite type of beer as it was all kegged beer. It was, however, decidedly not a hipster pub, so I was fine. As we walked in, we received a big smiley welcome from the lady behind the bar, and when I took a little interest in the guitar hanging from the wall, she stated that it was a well-used guitar and that I was welcome to have a go if I wanted. I played an instrumental piece and then put it back. As far as the clientele was concerned, this got off to a slow start. This is not a criticism, as we were there on a Monday evening when one would not expect much in the way of activity. As the evening wore on, a few people came in, one of which had two dogs in tow. I had brought a sketch pad with me and liked the look of the dogs, so I completed a very quick sketch of the two of them. The owner liked what she saw, so I gave it to her. By the end of the evening, everyone was posing for their portraits, and the whole pub was abuzz with conversation. It was a fun evening chatting about art with a regular who was himself an artist; music with a chap who was a professional musician; and, of course, beer. I would certainly go back there if this one visit were anything to go by.

The Bouncing Barrel, Herne Bay, Kent

Something I learned when I went into this pub for the first time. My family have lived in and around the stretch of coast that included Herne Bay to Margate for decades. I have therefore been going there for many years. I never knew that this stretch of coastline was used to test Mr Barnes-Wallace's bouncing bomb of Dambusters fame. The pub is named for this reason. It is an aeronautically themed – and specifically WW2 aeronautics – micropub. It has model aircraft hanging from the ceiling, pictures of aircraft on the walls and even the conversation, for some time, was RAF. It is very small, but when I walked in there, I found the welcome warm, the atmosphere friendly, and the beer good. It is all cask ale, and the demographic tends to be older in the off-season. I can't comment on the summer season as I have never been in there in the tourist season, but I am told it is bustling. I believe the pub advertises its closing time as 9 pm, but they are actually licensed to 11 pm and are just hedging their bets. If no one is in there after 9, they will close, but if they have a brisk trade, they will keep it going.

There is a sombre side note here. Emma, the lady who served us on our first visit and made our stay so welcoming sadly died during our second visit. She was not serving at the time but was ill in bed upstairs. We had become aware of a lack of staff during the evening. The owner then disappeared upstairs. He came down a short time later and asked everyone to finish their drinks and leave without explanation. None of us felt an explanation was required, we knew something had happened but kept our counsel and left. This is a pub that, similar to the Butcher's, prefers people to pay their bill at the end of the evening. The upshot of this policy was that no one was asked to pay their bill that day. I personally made contact when I had discovered what had happened, offered condolences and promised to pay on our next visit. they refused payment. The other issue they had was that they were in the middle of a beer festival and had eleven ales on cask. It is a vast amount to shift for a pub of that size, but they had to remain closed for the rest of Saturday and all of Sunday. So they sadly lost a good friend, an excellent employee and a significant amount of trade. My heart goes out to them.

The Pub, Herne Bay

First prize for the least imaginative pub name in the world goes to 'The Pub. In the age of t'internet, one can't put 'pub' in your internet search engine and expect people to find your establishment. But, hey-ho, them's the breaks. The pub interior is hardly inspiring either. Very bland and impersonal. The landlord, however, is neither bland nor unimaginative. I spoke at length to him and was Impressed by his perseverance, knowledge of the industry, and small but good range of beers. He tells me that when looking for premises to open his pub, he had to go through seven different applications for seven other premises before the licencing authority and the local authority relented. They all spout the same old lines that the community are concerned about drunkenness, disturbances, noise and general issues related to the sort of problems that the traditional pubs have always had. I have never been to a micropub that has ever had neighbours complaining about any of these issues. I have known several people who have gone through the same issues, and the authority normally relents but not without putting massive restrictions on the license. I can't help thinking that this is the pressure that is being put on by the bigger pubs who don't like the idea of new competition. These tiny pubs are frequented by the older end of our society. They have done all that rubbish, been to all those places and have a cupboard full of t-shirts. Little places like these do not cause problems. The Pub is undoubtedly one on my list of places to revisit – after I have settled up with the Bouncing Barrel.

The Pub, Ramsgate Kent

What can I say about this little gem (apart from the ludicrously unimaginative name)? I would love to go into the vibrant atmosphere created by the rich variety of people we met there. Unfortunately, I cannot. We went in there twice in one day. Once in the afternoon, when there was an international rugby match on, and everyone had stayed away to watch the game as there was no TV in the place. A fact that earns it extra brownie points, in my view. The second time was later in the evening when an event was on in a pub further up the road, which drew the regulars away. The result was that it was just my wife, the owner and me for the last hour or so. Before that, a few waifs and strays were dropping in on their way to the event. So no atmosphere, but I felt that a lot was going on and we had simply chosen the wrong day. The owner, a Bavarian lady with mixed English/German parentage, sat and chatted with us the entire time we were there. This was good. It gave me a sense of what she was about and where she was going with this little business. It is clearly a project she has delved into and is passionate about. She does have one Bavarian beer on. All the rest are English cask beers. There is a good range, and I am told that there will always be a dark beer on at all times of the year because she has a significant number of regulars that prefer that type. The décor is not fussy. She had the place renovated and found a stained-glass window above the door that had been covered up and an industrial-looking arch above where the bar is. These are now uncovered and part of the furniture. I am not sure why anyone would have covered it up in the first place. She has spent some money on the bar top. It was well made and solid. The walls were bare yellow brickwork, adding something to the place's general feel. Dogs were welcome, which is always a good signal for me. They even had a seat reserved for dogs which I thought was a good touch. Dogs were given treats with the customer's consent. All-in-all, we left there feeling quite good about the place. The owner knew where she was going with the place. She had a good knowledge of beer and the industry and seemed to work with the other local pubs rather than against them.

The Hovelling Boat Inn

We dropped into this little one after our first visit to The Pub. We were presented with a much busier establishment despite the rugby match—obviously not fans of the game in that pub. The space was much the same as The Pub, except that there was no bar. Beer was served directly from the stillage. There was a similar but different range of beers to The Pub. The atmosphere was much different due to the presence of people. There was something about the place that I was never sure of. There was no unpleasantness or anything like that, but I never really got into any conversations with anyone. There was a dog in there that was allowed to roam freely. I have no problem with that, although the dog was not obedient, and so, as an owner, I think I would have preferred it to have a little less freedom. I feel I am nit-picking with this point, but I am struggling to understand why I am not enthusing about the place. I would probably go back in there, if for no other reason than to give it a second chance. As far as I could see, it was not doing anything wrong, so it must be a good place to go. I think it would be a place to go on the way to The Pub.

The Just Reproach, Deal, Kent

Moving around the coastline to Deal. This town has several micropubs, but we decided on this one. The name is taken from a poem by Daniel Defoe called 'The Storm'. He clearly did not like this town one little bit. The last few lines go,

' The barbarous hated name of Deal should die

Or be a term of infamy

And until that's done, the town will stand

A just reproach to all the land'.

The pub itself is everything I like in a micro. It is small and cosy, the customers are friendly, the owner is friendly, and the beer range is excellent. When we first went in, we were served by a man who got our beers and started a tab. About 5 minutes later, a young Lady came in and took over from him. It turns out that he was a customer. He didn't work for the pub or have any financial interest in it. He was just helping out while the owner – the lady who had just come in, was on a mission of mercy. This told me a lot about the place. It boasted a very local group of regulars who were trusted enough by the owners to help out for 5 minutes here and there when, through no fault of their own, they had to absent themselves briefly.

There seemed to be a good flow of passing trade as well. There was the normal flow of conversation, and, as seems to be becoming the norm, everyone felt at ease conversing with complete strangers. The place has been going since 2011, so it is well established and long may it continue. I will return□

The Wilds of Surrey Calls

<u>The Real ALe Way</u>

If one trundles westward through Kent and into Surrey on the A25, a road that takes you from Sevenoaks to Guildford parallel to the southern stretch of the M25, you come across Westerham. A town remarkable for being so unremarkable. It seems to be a haunt of club cyclists, and on a warm summer's evening, they are there in force. Public transport links are okay if you don't want public transport links. I ran an internet search on this subject using Westerham as a starting point; the computer advised a taxi to the next town along. Never mind, there is a pub called the Real Ale Way (now sadly closed permanently, although the owners have two more in the Kent area of Greater London). We sort of happened upon it one day during midweek and decided to pop in. Good selection of beer, and the locals were chatty, so I felt at home. Then without warning, a small acoustic band descended and entertained us for the evening. We meet all sorts in there on our occasional trips in that direction: carpenters, plumbers, lawyers, American Spitfire pilots. Although I suppose everyone meets American spitfire pilots in micropubs all the time.

Being sad at the loss of the Westerham Branch of the Real Ale Way, we thought we should explore their other outlets. I have to say it was a somewhat inauspicious day to choose for this short odyssey. As the name suggests, there is a railway theme there. That theme seems to be being in close proximity to a railway station. Westerham was the exception having no railway station. They now have one on Station approach next to Hayes Station and one on Station Road in West Wickham. These are two towns that no one really goes to as a destination. They either pass through it or they go there for a specific reason. As a result, I don't really know the areas very well. Being close to railway stations is a good place to start a pub because you have good passing trade from people coming home from work and popping in for a swift half before dinner. As it happens, I am told there is a definite trend towards doing just this and then returning after dinner to finish off. The time, to get back to my point was inauspicious because there was a train strike on the day we decided to go. So much for being good places to start pubs. They were both some ten or more miles from my home, so it was not a straightforward journey. We had plumped for the Hayes branch for no particular reason. This meant alternative forms of transport. We worked out a route that involved a tram journey followed by a bus ride. We had not considered the other one in West Wickham, but I decided to see exactly where it was as we trundled down the road on the 119 bus. I found a postcode and entered that into the maps programme on my phone and found that it was a three-minute walk from our current location. We swiftly decided to change our minds and go with this one in West Wickham.

We were not disappointed. On entering, we found a busy pub with a good range of beers from Kent. I was not sure that I was going to get my normal conversation going, but two minutes later, we were off and running and had a thoroughly entertaining evening chatting with a retired postmaster who was clearly not only a regular but someone who was born and bred in the area. To me, it was very unusual as it appeared to have a very large core of local customers who all seemed to know each other. Pubs on main roads in London don't tend to have this; they tend to rely almost exclusively on passing trade. The bar staff were referring to the customers using their first names and seemed to know each individual's tastes. It had the feel of a small town micro – which is not a bad thing in my experience. We will have to return and try the Hayes Branch when the trains are behaving themselves, but I have a good feeling about it.

We can't spend all week there, so a short hop through the North Downs area of Surrey into Whyteleafe and my next pub.

 **Radius Arms, Whyteleafe, Surrey**

Whyteleafe is the last town before the M25 (motorway that surrounds London) when driving out of London to the south. It's a small town with not a lot going on. People need to go into nearby Caterham to the west or Purley to the North to do any shopping. The one thing it does have is a micro called The Radius Arms. Now pedants will be jumping up and down about the name. The word 'arms' relate to a coat of arms. Coats of arms are like modern-day logos. They are designed mainly for royalty, aristocratic families and trade organisations. So pubs with this word included in their names were named either for the local aristocrat, the royal family, or to represent trade organisations such as blacksmiths, wheelwrights and such like. Obviously, 'Radius' doesn't fall into any of these slots, so it is technically incorrect. But do you know what? Due to this unforgivable linguistic error, the world hasn't stopped turning on its axis. I've had hardly any sleepless nights pondering this problem . . . actually, I haven't had any. The pub is a really good little place to go, and the customers and publican are good people. So, I don't care about the semantics.

The pub seats about 24 or so people inside and a few tables outside to allow for overflow. It has a good range of cask and keg ales. It is as far from hipster as you can get, so the prices are reasonable. There is only one toilet, but there is no need to queue as there is a light outside that shines green when empty and red when engaged. Vince, the owner, who had a previous life as a bus driver, is not the most talkative of people. I get the impression that he is pretty shy, but he keeps a good house, so I don't mind. You know he makes a positive impact when one of his regulars, who is profoundly blind, is able to walk up to the bar and have a chat with Vince and the regulars without having to ask to whom he is speaking. He recognises people by their voices. The regulars simply say hello to him, and that is enough for him to know who is in there.

They have a bit of a community get-together every Sunday when everyone brings sharing food. I'm not sure how this goes down at home when the Sunday dinner is being prepared while half the household is gorging themselves on morsels of snacking treats at the pub, but I like the idea.

I have, in the past, taken a pencil and paper into some pubs. I sometimes get the urge to draw pictures. I did this one day in the Radius and ended up drawing a caricature of Vince and his assistant. I would generally screw the drawing up so no one knows what has happened. My wife, however, will steal some of them off me and hand them over to the subject of my scratchings. This very small, very rough sketch now has pride of place on the wall in the pub and is featured in their 2021 calendar—fame at last.

A few short miles in towards the outskirts of Croydon is another Micropub, The Golden Ark, that was opened by another ex-bus driver. I don't know; you wait for one micropub to come for ages and ages, and then two come at the same time! (a little London in-joke). It is a little off the beaten track for it to be a regular of mine, but a fine pub in the best traditions of this new phenomenon, the micropub. It has a good range of beers, friendly, knowledgeable staff. We sat there one evening when a person, who I would describe as either southern European or mixed-race Asian, sat at our table and started talking to us quite randomly. It soon became apparent that she was the owner's wife and just came over to chat. I like that there is also a friend who lives nearby, so handy if I want a catch-up.

 **Cobbett's, Dorking, Surrey**

A further jaunt down the A25 from Westerham toward Guildford will see you in Dorking. It is an unassuming 'middle England' town (in the parochial rather than the geographical sense) in the wilds of deepest Surrey. It is far enough away from the larger towns of Guildford, Horsham and London for it not to bother the locals too much but close enough to commute easily. Just off the main shopping street is Cobbett's. The premises was a beer shop that only had a licence to sell alcohol for consumption off the premises (an off licence). He had a good and varied range of local beers and built a name for himself. He then started selling draught beers to take away. He allowed people to taste before they bought, and these tasting sessions became more and more drawn out. He became more popular, so he obtained an on-licence, and people came in, bought a pint, and browsed around the shop. One of his regulars suggested putting chairs in a small room in the back. When I say small, we are talking about seating for ten people with a couple standing and a further six outside in what is loosely described as a beer garden. A tall man standing in the middle can almost touch both walls with outstretched arms. This suggestion was acted upon, and the place has slowly morphed into a micropub with an off-licence instead of an off-licence with a micropub if that makes any sense. There is now also a table and chairs in the main shop area that will seat four.

Once again, this is not a hipster pub. It has sold, until recently, a full range of cask and kegged beers. Strangely, its takeaway alcohol seems to be more expensive, but I don't go there for that, so I may be inaccurate here. Whenever there is a folk music event in the town, Cobbetts gets packed out because folk music and beer seem to be inextricably linked. It's too small for the musicians to strike up or dancers to dance, so they just come to relax and talk to each other. Because it is such a small room, there are no private conversations. You either get involved in the chat or sit there and say nothing. I once used Cobbett's as a place to meet an old-school friend who I had not met in over 40 years. I thought it turned out to be a good evening. I wasn't aware, but before I suggested the venue, there had a folky event organised for that day, so it was quite fun reminiscing among a load of other people, some, but not many of whom I didn't know. My long-lost friend is also a musician, so he felt at home.

This pub closes at 8pm every day, probably reflecting its off-licence past. I don't have a problem with this because I am aware of the times, so I plan for them. The last two times I have been there, my wife and I went for a long walk and arrived there earlier than I would typically go to a pub but gasping for a pint never-the-less. I was sufficiently refreshed by the time I left.

Having said all this, since writing this review, I have recently visited this pub and found that people are noticing a concerning trend away from cask ales. When I was there earlier this year, they only had two middle-of-the-road pale ales, the only difference between them being that one was a cloudy beer. Then later, at the beginning of summer, only one undrinkable cask beer was on. This cloudiness is a new trend where the brewer does not go through the process of clearing the beer. It appears that having one less thing to do makes the beer more expensive, and I don't like that. It is more expensive as it is seen as more trendy. I am not trendy. With Cobbetts trending away from cask ales, they are starting to charge more for these pretty average beers that they don't have to look after. It seems that I can get better beer in many other places at much more reasonable prices. I hope this trend is halted, but I don't think it will. It is easier to keep kegged beer; you don't have to look after it nearly as much as cask ales.

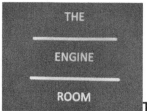

The Engine Room

We will now geographically back-track a little and pootle down the A22, a road that runs between Purley, to the South of Croydon and Eastbourne on the south coast. Somewhere roughly halfway along, one comes across East Grinstead. The name of this town, for reasons I can't understand, evokes images of grime and hardship. This is not what one is presented with on arrival. It is an altogether unremarkable, middle England East Sussex town leading from an uninteresting place – Purley – to another uninteresting place – Eastbourne. It is perfectly pleasant, and the surrounding area is very English – rolling hills and leafy lanes. On our first arrival, we were utterly disappointed because a micropub that we were aiming for was not worth the drive down, and we were expecting to have a dry night. We decided to try and find somewhere else in town. We succeeded – with knobs on.

Our first issue was finding the place. You could walk up and down the High Street until you are dizzy and still not find it if you are looking for something that resembles anything you would willingly walk into. The observant pub seekers – of which I am evidently not one – will spot a sign on a wall at the entrance of a somewhat grimy-looking alleyway. If one looks down this alleyway, one's hopes are not assuaged. There appears to be nothing that looks like a retail outlet, and there is no reason that anyone would go down there for honest purposes. But the sign is there, and so one must try. In for a penny, in for a pound. At the end of the alleyway is a door to the left of what appears to be a beer garden without a pub. When you walk through the door, you find a TV monitor with a list of beers, ciders and gins. No bar, no seating, no people. Just a TV monitor. The beer list is enough to spur us on, so in we go, down a corridor, round a corner. Past a small enclave with a couple of people having a drink. Then the signs for a toilet in one direction and an arrow with the words, 'to the bar'. And voila! A pub.

Seating for four people. In the bar area. No seating at the bar and a spectacular list of cask and kegged ales and gins for every taste. There are little enclaves dotted around the place outside the bar so that there is plenty of room. The only way I get a conversation with the locals is to sit in the bar area. But this is fine. It can be a little weird if one isn't aware that there are other places to sit. Sitting in this tiny pub with a seemingly endless flow of people who seem to come from nowhere and disappear with their beers until their glasses need to be recharged.

They somehow manage to have live unplugged music in there. I have never been there when this has happened, so I can't work out how they do it. I am aware that they have quiz nights where the quizmaster has a mic that feeds into all the little rooms. It apparently works very well, but I can't see how that would work for music. I will have to check it out soon. They also have a Christmas raffle which we decided to support by buying three tickets. Two came up trumps, and we were allowed to choose our prizes. Fortunately, there were two £20 vouchers for the Engine room, so we took those and invited some friends along to help us use them up. We did so, and some. It was a rather wobbly morning the next day.

This place advertises itself on some social media platforms as a brewery tap. This is how they started life, but I believe the brewery no longer does its stuff, so this needs to be revised. This doesn't detract from the fact that it is a great little place, and we will happily go to East Grinstead just to go there.☐

The West

A little trundle down the Jurassic coast will take you to some delightful places. Unfortunately, there are too many, so we tend to bypass many of these little towns. A recent trip to see an old friend who was visiting from Australia brought us to this part of our universe. We were due to meet her on Wednesday, but ever the enthusiast, we decided to head out on the Tuesday and see what we could discover. For those not certain of the topography, the Jurassic coast is the south coast of Dorset County. It has plenty of little towns and larger cities, most of which rely absolutely on summer tourism.

Weymouth was our first port of call. Many people tell me that this is a charming town. I must say that I thought it was pretty unremarkable. I judge towns by their high streets first. After that, I look for the little nuances that make these places different. I was only there for a day, so my view is not steeped in knowledge. The High Street was every other Highstreet in England. Dull, uninspiring, full of 'same-ole-same-ole' bland chain stores, charity shops and betting shops.

Then there was the pub. We had travelled 120 miles and ended up going into a pub called the Dog House, and one that was a Hopback Brewery-tied pub. I have a Dog House and a Hopback pub that are both within a four-mile walk of where I live. Oh well, here we go.

The Dog House, Weymouth, Dorset

Weymouth's first and only Micropub. You walk in there and are met by a very friendly but intense Border Collie called Ruddles – the pub dog. We then entered a long, narrow space with a bar at the end. Given that this was the last day in February, so definitely not tourist season, I had to forgive the fact that it was not exactly overflowing. We wandered in and settled down to a very pleasant beer, if a little on the strong side. Then the inevitable conversation is started. All the other customers had drifted off, leaving my wife and I and one other, Mark. It seems he grew up around Carshalton and was friends or acquaintances with many people we knew. He knew our local traditional pub – the Hope (subject of an entry hereinafter) – and all the people who run it. We were able to talk at length and what was going on in the area and who was doing what, when and where. This is why I like these places so much. One hundred twenty miles from home, I'm talking to a stranger who knows my friends. So, having exhausted that subject, we mentioned that we had recently been to Herne Bay. "Oh," says he, "I go there regularly. Have you been to the Bouncing Barrel?" Well, if the reader is not skipping through chapters, you will remember a previous entry in this very tome. He was, of course, aware of who Emma was but not what had happened, so we were able to let him know.

So, one person, who we had never met, sitting in a pub we had never been to, knew two pubs that we enjoyed going to. One was 120 miles from where we were seated, and the other 200 miles.

As far as the pub is concerned, I would be reluctant to comment at length as I have only been there once during the off-season in a town that hibernates for the first three months of the year. They had a good range of beer – dark and light, weak and strong – served from stillage. The owner appeared to be knowledgeable and well-informed. I found the weekday opening hour odd. Noon to 7 pm. I'm sure he knows his customers, and these are his best hours; they just are unusual.

The All Hail Ale and the Porterhouse, Westbourne, Dorset

Then we are off to Bournemouth. Or, more accurately, a satellite town to the north called Westbourne and the All Hail Ale micropub and the Porterhouse. The latter was difficult to figure out. I couldn't decide whether it was a small pub or a micro. It matters not. If it's a good pub, it's a good pub. This one was not particularly exciting. The beer range was local, but all middle-of-the-road, dull beers. It did have a traditional feel to the place. The former was better, though hardly memorable. Ten days after visiting there, I can't remember a thing about it for the life of me, and we were fairly sober when we left there. I fear the following comments are based on a conference with my wife to try to jog my memory.

Memory jogged! This is a bit of a hipster pub that does a few cask ales. The fizz was, as ever, over-priced, with some coming in at over £10 a pint. No thanks. Looking at the bewildering list of fizz, I had to chuckle. They all had weird and wonderful names with prices for half pints and pints. The one that caught my attention was a dark beer that was yours for a mere £8.30 a pint or £4.00 for half. Were I the sort to drink this rubbish, I think I may have asked for two half pints and an empty pint glass. I have never been parsimonious, but the opportunity would be too tempting to miss. My adult side felt the need to point out the error, but my puerile, mischievous side won over.

The cask ale was good, with a good range of light and dark. It was also reasonably priced. All the tables had pub games, including Kerplunk, backgammon, scrabble and other pub favourites. I did not get the feeling that it was the sort of pub that one would expect to have a good conversation, although it had a bit of a 'local pub' feel to it, which in my world, is a big tick in the pro's box. All in all, it is a pub in which I would be happy to spend an evening, but it was not the sort of pub I would travel 100 miles to go to without having other reasons to be there, which, on this occasion, I did.

Art Brew late of Sutcoombe Devon

Now, I want to take you on a trip west. We delight in finding new pubs on our mini tours in the camper van. We often find out-of-the-way little gems. North Devon came into our purview when we were looking for a small campsite to stay for a night or two. This one couldn't get more out-of-the-way or little. Just outside a little village called Sutcoombe, a small campsite was attached to an even smaller Microbrewery, which had an even smaller micropub. The Brewery is Art Brew, a tiny two-barrel that seems to move on a fairly regular basis. I suppose that, with such a small brewery, one would just have to shove it into your backpack and wander off at a moment's notice. He does, however, have some prize-winning beers. They are well made kegged beers. His pricing was the simplest I have ever known. £3 a pint of beer or large wine, £1.50 for half a pint of small wine. £2 for small prosecco. No charge for soft drinks for the designated driver. His opening hours were even more straightforward. A sign outside the pub proclaimed that the pub opened at 6 pm on Friday and noon on Saturday. He lived directly across the narrow country road that separated the house from the brewery. He would therefore sit at the window with a cup of tea and open up when the first customer arrived. And he closed when the last one left. The other thing about this brewery was that the owner was distinctly left-wing in his political outlook, not that he made a thing of it or encouraged political debate. His logo is a little bland but does use one symbol that was something of a giveaway; it was very similar to the anarchist logo—it made me chuckle. Whenever we went there after, he would insist that I bring a mandolin or a guitar, he would get other customers to do the same, and an impromptu jam sesh would start. The brewery has now moved on to Reading and seems to pop up here and there at random times.

It was a 'tour', so we had to move on from there. In so doing, we found a pub in Llandrindod Wells. For those who don't go there much, Wales seems to consist of the 'friendly' bit on the south coast and the not-so-friendly bit on the north coast. Everything in the middle is just a means of transit between two the ends. Aberystwyth is on the west coast because someone had to put something there. This view is obviously wrong. There is life in the middle, and Llandrindod Wells is one. It boasts the first ever motor vehicle in Wales, a Benz 1899 model (for the more astute, this was before Benz met Daimler and his daughter Mercedes). The vehicle is still operational to this day, although not in Llandrindod wells. The town also had a little Micropub, which called itself Arvon Ales. It served a good range of reasonably priced beers. It was friendly and comfortable. When we went in there, we got talking, as we often do and found two people who had been to our local pubs in South London. It fascinates me that we are constantly finding these physically distant but nevertheless, close connections wherever we go.

It is an easy drive to the Welsh/English border, where you will find Ludlow in Shropshire, so if the aggressive Welsh hoards felt the need to drive you out of their country, civilisation is not too far, and Ludlow is one of my favourite towns in England. It has a food festival every year that is a must for anyone who likes food. There are a couple of Micropubs there, but we always seem to get there when they are closed, so I couldn't comment on them as I started writing this. But hey, this is a developing story. Fast forward circa one year, and we are on another tour. We make an effort to avoid Tuesday, as this appears to be the day that Ludlow goes to sleep. Our arrival was timed for Wednesday. One rather nasty headache later, I was able to regale all with my experiences and have reproduced it at the end of this section of the book that deals with micropubs.

South through Herefordshire, and we are now in Ross-on-Wye near the Welsh border. It's our first visit to the town. I like the area as a whole. It has stunning countryside. It is miles from the nearest major metropolitan area, and life seems a little less frenetic than I am used to. The second time we went there, lockdown was just easing, and Wales had much more stringent rules. We did have a chuckle, though, when, as we were going for a stroll, a middle-aged woman approached us and asked which country we were in. A seemingly strange question if you weren't aware of the proximity of the Welsh border. 'England', we declared, and she thanked us, removed her face mask, and went about her business. Two minutes later, a younger, similar-looking woman approached us and asked precisely the same question. We did explain why we burst out laughing. She said, 'Oh, that'll be my mother. How long ago was that? I'm trying to catch up with her.'

On our first visit, we were aware of a micropub in the town and wished to seek it out. We located it opposite a huge supermarket on the edge of the town centre.

The Tap House, Ross-on-Wye, Herefordshire

We were not aware of how long this pub had been going. We were surprised that it was two weeks old. We walked in there and found a small area that seated sixteen to twenty. There was a good range of cask and kegged beer and a lady at the bar looking slightly concerned. It turned out that the toilet had spectacularly failed, and her husband was tearing around like a man demented trying to get it sorted out. They could not open the pub unless they could offer toilet facilities. She then seemed to look off into the distance for a moment and then said, 'Actually, there's a huge supermarket across the road. They have plenty of toilets. There! I have offered toilets facilities, so I can open the pub. What Can I do for you?' we have been going back there ever since. Every time I am somewhere near, I wander in. I even told Nigel, the licensee, that I was only going to be in the area the following Monday on one of our mini-tours. He doesn't normally open on Monday, but he did so for us. He was able to call on some of his other customers so that he had a reasonable number in there, but he pulled the stops for us..

Coming out of lockdown, we were restricted in terms of pub visits and had to book and reserve a table. For us, this meant that spontaneity had to be forfeited. We still managed some pretty cool days, one of which was in the Tap House. We were on a bit of a beer tour and had booked a table several days earlier. When we got there, he showed us into a side room that I wasn't even aware existed. He showed us to our table, and we took our seats. In the room were two other couples at two other tables. None of us had met, and we were all from out of town. A conversation inevitably started. Typically there is something that triggers it, and, on this occasion, one of the ladies had a Southern African accent. My wife hails from the same part of the world, so this was a way in. It turns out that both came from Zimbabwe. He was a folk musician who played music for Morris's dancing sides. I am a folk musician who plays for a local Morris dancing side. They both live in Herne Bay – where my sister lives – and frequented the previously featured Butcher's Arms. This conversation is going well. There is so much going on between the four of us, given that we had never met. Then the chap at the other table piped up. His story had so many parallels to my life story it was barely credible. He was born in India and spent the first seven years of his life moving around, never settling down in any school. I was born in Scotland and moved around for the first seven years of my life (RAF Brat). He found himself in Kenya in central Africa circa 1968. I landed in Africa on 24th June 1968. He left Africa and came to England in 1983, as did I. He now owns a motorhome and roams around England as often as he can. As do I. We now have three couples who have never met but who have definite connections. We were in the process of marvelling about this when a seventh person wandered in. None of us took to him much, but he told us that he lived in Ross-on-Wye, but he came from South Wimbledon, and his local pub was our current local, The Trafalgar. So never mind your 'six degrees of separation'. There weren't even two between the seven of us.

The picture at the head of this passage is not the logo for the pub but the microbrewery to which it is attached. I believe the brewery came sometime after the pub. The brewery I know very little about. It is called the Motley Hog and is named thus, as a member of the rock group the Mott the Hoople came from the area and came in and had a few drinks there once. I believe the symbol for Ross-on-Wye is the hedgehog.

Cider Barn

The cider barn was a fabulous little find. It is in a small place called Draycott, about a 45-minute walk from Cheddar in the Mendips of Somerset. A place where one can blow a month's wages on cheese alone – or just go to your local supermarket and buy exactly the same product for a quarter of the price because you don't have the kudos of having bought it from its source. We were on our travels around England looking for different interesting pubs and towns, and this part of the country had an embarrassment of riches. We had never been to Cheddar and thought it would be about the right time. We found a campsite and booked in. The Cider Barn is, as the name states, a cider pub in a converted barn. It has a couple of ales, but it is mainly cider. We rolled in there one Sunday afternoon, not expecting much, only to find many people carrying various musical instruments and accoutrements. It soon became apparent that they had about five different acts, all starting about 30 minutes after we got there. So we had a day of good live music, conversation and beer. The wife stuck to cider. I then heard that they had little jam sessions mid-week, and the next one was the following Wednesday. I rearranged our schedule so that we could return on the said Wednesday armed with a guitar. Another good evening was had by all.

Brewing Co Totnes

Totnes is one of those delightful little towns that have decided they don't want big multinationals clogging up the town centre. Much better to have small independent shops full of different one-off products. There was a small pub in the town that had its own single-barrel brewery behind the bar. I thought it was a good touch. I have only been there once, so I can't say too much about the place, but I liked the enterprise.

The Folk Scene

The folk scene, Morris's dancing and battle re-enactments and campanology all have one thing that binds them together. Beer. As a musician for a Morris dancing side, I get to go to several folk festivals throughout the year.

Hastings Jack-in-the-Green is an ancient tradition that was forgotten about for centuries and brought back to life a few decades ago. It is a spring festival that takes place on the weekend that incorporates the first Monday of May each year. Extra events are added when the 1st of May falls on that weekend, and even more so when, as next year (2023) will bear witness, it falls on a Monday. Hastings is the home of two Micropubs and a number of other traditional pubs, all of whih are good places to go to listen to music and drink decent beer.

First In Last out, Hastings, East Sussex

First In Last Out (FILO) is up the hill close to the centre of the old town. It has its own brewery and brews a reasonable range, if not the most exciting beers. It is always on the menu when we go there, but there are many good venues, so it isn't a case of going there, settling down for the weekend and not going anywhere. Any pub that can make a living among a bunch of very good venues has to be doing something right. It has a decent amount of seating and a room in the back that is a bit bland but somewhere to sit, nevertheless. I have never really found this to be a pub where I could comfortably strike up a conversation with a random customer as I can in other pubs. I tend to go there with my group of dancers, and this may be the reason, or it may be something else, I don't know.

The Jolly Fisherman, Hastings, East Sussex

The Jolly Fisherman is a newly opened pub that we wandered into at the last Jack-in-the-Green. It seemed very good but so jam-packed that they were queuing out the door to get beer. Not that we had to wait long. The staff were good and people were served in good time so everyone was happy. The beer quality was also in their favour, so somewhere to investigate. To that end, we returned there recently to check it out when the Jack-in-the-Green multitudes were elsewhere. We dropped in mid-afternoon on a Saturday and immediately started chatting to someone who recognised us from Jack in the Green. We only stayed for one but returned later that evening. It is the nature of micropubs that, if it is busy, people expect you to take seat at a table even if there are already people sitting there. This was the situation that evening and through the course of the evening we helped someone with their GK crossword and had conversations with a CAMRA stalwart and two gentlemen who had been on a pub crawl all day. There were two cask beer and a load of Kegged stuff. I am told that the licensee tends towards the kegged stuff in the winter to avoid too much ullage. We shall see come May.

There are other micropubs opening all the time, and Hastings has its fair share. It is a town full of music and art and people looking to have an outlet for it or just to come and see or hear what is on offer. I am certain that when I return, there will be at least one other pub to check out.

In land from there you will find Tenterden in Kent. They have an annual folk festival full of singing and dancing both in the street and in pubs and other venues. Most of the pubs there are fairly standard work-a-day pubs. They do, however, have a small brewery. The Old Dairy which was built on the site of an old agricultural venture. My highly developed detective skills tell me that it was a dairy, but you never know. The beers are not normally my thing. They don't do much in the way of dark beers and the light ones are generally well made but unexciting. Green hop season, which is around the time when Hops are being harvested and breweries snap up fresh hops that go from the farm into the vat within a day of collection. These beers are normally to my taste on the lighter spectrum, and Old Dairy do two. A session, low ABV and a slightly strong one. These do not disappoint, but if there is a dark beer around, I would probably go with that. It has a tap room and has one of the best jam sessions I have been to with sea shanties being sang a cappella, and all manner of instrumental folk songs and tunes.

Moving on towards the East Coast of Kent, we find Sandwich. Another folk festival much earlier in the year. We went there for the first time in 2022 and I was quite disappointed with the pub choice. There were only two that I had any interest in. One traditional pub and one micro.

 **Smuggler's Beer and Music Café, Sandwich, Kent**

This hidden gem, hiding in plain sight in the town centre, a stone's throw away from the other decent pub, is a really good find. We went in there during their weeklong folk festival. It would seat around 20 people, and when we went in there, there was a mic set up for music. They were expecting a couple to come in and entertain the masses that evening. The lady behind the bar, who I think was one of the owners, was on her own, and although it wasn't bursting at the seams, she had not been able to have a break all day. She had been on the go without a break for over twelve hours by the end of the night.

Our group of dancers descended on the pub and settled in for the evening. Having seen how much she was struggling and having, within our group, people who have spent their lives in the pub trade, we found ourselves helping her out, changing barrels and the like, just to give her a break. Then the musicians didn't show up, so some customers looked a little disappointed. Once again, we, the knights in shining tatters, well equipped with various musical instruments, came to the rescue and started an impromptu folk session. This helped the owner in two ways. First, the fee for the musicians did not have to be paid – we do it for free – and the customers were delighted and stuck around to put money over her counter. We had our drinks paid for throughout the night by the customers, and everyone was joining in where they could. Other musicians started wandering in, and it turned into a very good evening. At the end of the evening, we helped out closing up and walked off happy. We went back in there the next day. She had her daughters in to help this time but was so pleased to see us that she booked us in for next year to do the same. We'll be there, of that you can be assured, given that our dance group has also been invited back for the folk festival.

Mind The Gap

The first pub we went to in this town was Mind the Gap. A clear reference to the railway announcements that remind everyone to do the obvious when boarding or alighting trains. There is, of course, going to be a railway theme to the pub, which is fine, but strangely no railway-themed logo and a very bland frontage, hence no thumbnail picture at the top of the paragraph. This pub has two distinct sections, a seating area that seats sixteen to twenty people, then up a short flight of stairs in what seems to be halfway between a mezzanine level and a 'split-level' single floor. On this raised level stands the bar with some limited seating in a limited area, especially when it is busy, and people need to get past to answer the call of nature, which is in that part of the premises. The pub boasts a good range of cask and kegged beers for most tastes. They like to have live music there, which is always fine by me. Not sure about having hard rock cover groups in such a small space – which was what we were presented with at the last folk festival – but if It works for them, I'm okay with that. I know they have smaller unplugged gigs there as well. I was a little disappointed with the service when this rock group were performing, as the staff, which included the licensee, seemed more interested in the music than the customers. That is my one criticism of a pub that does good things. It won't stop me from going there unless that becomes an ongoing issue.

The Magnet Micropub

The second micro we found was the Magnet. A little larger than most, but intimate nevertheless. It is situated in the town centre and has a good passing trade as well as a strong local clientele. I was quite impressed by the speed of service when it was bursting at the seams at the last folk festival. There wasn't anywhere to sit, but that is what you get with little pubs—a good range of beers and live music. I had never been there when there has not been a folk festival, so I couldn't really comment further initially. It has all the elements I like but requires further investigation. To this end, I recently went there while investigating local micros in the area. This was the bleak midwinter, and it was rather cold out. The pub was warm and welcoming with their usual good range of beers. We immediately struck up a conversation with a man wearing an American civil war confederate hat. In the front was a trio of musicians with the oddest collection of instruments; A Spanish guitar, a Sousaphone and a piano/accordion. Each musician was very good at what they did, so they worked well together and produced a good eclectic array of tunes. This pub did not disappoint in terms of atmosphere, beer range, prices, and customer service.

The Chapel

This place has neither the look nor the feel of a religious establishment. It is a quirky little place that serves a decent selection of real ales and lagers. It has a small front room where everyone gathers, and behind this is the larger room that houses the rather long bar. It had friendly staff who were happy to pour beer directly into our own beer tankards as long as they held more than a pint. The last time we went in there, there were only two beers on. I gather that this is because it was midwinter in a town that relies on summer for survival. So a much-reduced footfall means either more ullage or put fewer cask beers on. The latter is the more sensible option.

THE ROYSTON the Royston, Broadstairs, Kent

On our last folk festival, we had finished prancing around for the day and had gone back to the campsite to get changed before painting the town red for the evening, as a bunch of people with an age range of between 24 and 70 are wont to do on these occasions. We were pootling along walking towards Mind the Gap when one of my companions and I looked right and found another pub that was not known to us before. Being diligent researchers of refreshment houses, we felt it would be a dereliction of duty not to go in there and sample their product. Again, I had never been to this pub when there wasn't a folk festival, so I didn't know how that would impact . Having said that, it is far enough away from the main melee that it either wasn't being affected or it was being negatively impacted in terms of footfall. This didn't detract from the good beer, good atmosphere and comfortable surroundings that we found on our first day. The warm welcome we received when we returned the next day spoke clearly that this was a place to which I would return. Because of its location, I get the impression that it would rely quite heavily on local trade rather than tourist footfall or passing trade, even in the tourist season. The main tourist area is only a ten-minute walk, but it is away from the town centre, the beach and the seaside attractions. This, to me, is a plus. On our second day there, when I arrived, my team were already there, and a young adult man was sitting with them. I didn't take long to realise that he had a mild mental disorder, so when two others approached and sat with us, we started suspecting that the latecomers were somewhat shady characters who were using the young chap for nefarious reasons. There was no evidence, so we could do nothing official, but we shared our concerns with the bar staff. They were wary of these others and were already keeping an eye open for the young guy's welfare—a big tick in their community engagement box.

And there's more?

This pub phenomenon has really been gaining traction over the last 10 to 15 years. It is, therefore, a very new concept. Because of this, it is in a constant state of flux. Pubs are opening and closing as fast as you can count them. Some are even there for short periods quite deliberately. This is the 'pop-up' generation, where all sorts of shops and food outlets can open for limited periods at relatively low overheads. Many are only there for short periods despite what the owners have desired and have closed down for a whole range of reasons. Having said this, I am always interested when new ones open near me. I get to check them out and support their endeavours. But only if they are doing a good job. Because of this, I go into a number of these places once or twice only. Sometimes it is just because they are off the beaten track, and I can't justify trekking out miles just to go to one pub. Sometimes it is just that they don't sell the product I want, and sometimes they are just too expensive. No one minds a reasonable markup; in fact, most of us expect it. The owners aren't there for their health, after all. What we don't like is huge markups because it's the trendy thing to do.

The Larkins Alehouse

Larkins Ale House, Cranbrook in Kent, is one such place that is just too far away to make it a viable journey. It is a perfectly good ale house with a good selection of beers catering to a small town in Kent. Its customers are, by and large, locals because, although it is on the main road, it is a small village that people tend to bypass on the way to or from Tonbridge or Maidenhead. There is not much passing trade there. There was a little confusion the first time we went as the door was shut and locked even though there were people within. We tentatively knocked on the door and were allowed access without question. It turned out that the local travelling community were in town celebrating a funeral or some such event. This particular group had a reputation as being troublesome, with a few drinks under their belts. Although the pub was very small and not what they would have been looking for, the owners had fallen foul of allowing too much rope in the past. They were therefore monitoring people to make sure they weren't going to upset their quiet little drinking hole. I don't think it was aimed entirely at the travelling community, just rowdy people of whom this particular group had plenty to spare. I wonder what they would have thought if they had known we were staying in a camper van in their town overnight.

We now move back to Margate. As Thanet seems to have shooed away all the camper van users, we have had to be a little more creative when going to that part of the world. Although they will never admit it, it appears that Margate has a problem for one weekend a year with a group of young bucks in souped-up gas-guzzlers ripping up the road, parking all over the manicured lawns at the side of the road and leaving litter lying around for the local residents to trip over on their morning seaside strolls. This is a display of complete disregard for the rule of law, the local neighbours and the showing of fundamental human thoughtlessness. This happens for just one weekend a year in August, and people's lives are made a misery for those two days. Especially at night. So what does one do about a group who have no regard for the law or its practitioners? Make up another rule! That should sort them out. Because they will see that they aren't allowed to do this and go home to bed. Or maybe not. But how do they make this rule? There is a distinct possibility that many are from the travelling community. I can imagine the conversation in the council office meetings: We don't want to target them specifically. That would be racist. We can't stop everyone from parking on the specific roads that are affected because that would wind up the locals. I know! Travelling people all live in campervans, so we will ban campervans from parking there in the evening. But how do we explain why? There has to be a reason, and we can't be racist. We will just say that campervans are dangerous and obstructive and cause litter. It doesn't matter that you could get articulated lorries four abreast down that street, it is so wide. We will just have to brush over that.

So it is that the motorhome-owning community have been made unwelcomed to Thanet. This community is made up of 45 - 70-year-old retired or semi-retired people who do not tend to play loud rock music at 3 am and urinate on people's doorsteps. They certainly don't rev up their engines and tear up the manicured lawns along the Royal Esplanade. These are people who have a little money to spend in their towns, and they have been moved along to go and spend their money elsewhere. In the meantime, they still have the same problem. That hasn't been solved. They still have young oiks annoying the residents once a year. the obstructions caused by the vehicles was never there anyway and litter? RV owners have their own waste disposal systems and the vast amounts of litter caused by day trippers who don't have RVs would eclipse any waste issues by a distance. All they have done is put less money into the shops and pubs of the towns. If it weren't for family issues, I wouldn't go there.

Unfortunately, I do, so I will go to Margate. I will stay as long as I have to, then go elsewhere. Whitstable is still in Thanet, but it isn't Margate, and they do have a good selection of pubs. We found one such pub in Tankerton, a suburb of Whitstable, on the way to Herne Bay. It is the

Tankerton Arms and has all the things that I like about a small pub. As it is away from Whitstable town centre, they tend to rely on the local customer base, so it is not all that seasonal as some of these seaside places can be. It is small, unpretentious and has a good selection of cask and kegged ale.

We have also been in the Black Dog and the Twelve Taps in Whitstable town Centre. Both good town centre pubs and places to which I will return. Having only been in them once, I can't comment further. I have noticed that there is an online 'Micropub Magazine.' This lists 72 micropubs in Kent alone, and I am reasonably sure that there are many

 The Dog House, Croydon Surrey

The Dog House is the newest pub, having been open for about three months as I write this piece. It is the third pub on my bus run. I first met Phil, the licensee, when I was in the Radius Arms circa February 2022. Vince, who had been helping him out and showing him the ropes in anticipation of opening his own pub, introduced him to me as he was aware that I lived locally to the proposed location. It's about four miles (6.3km), but that is local enough for me. I kept an eye open for this new pub for the next few months. I noticed that there were objections to a new pub in the area, probably from the big pub a stone's throw away from the site of the new pub, because they were worried about losing customers. As it is a pretty ropey pub, I would be worried as well, but here is an idea: try improving yours first rather than stopping other people from carrying on their own business.

The Dog House, on the border between Croydon and Wallington boroughs of South London, probably is taking some of the big pub's customers, but that is only because he is trying to keep a good house. In any case, it finally got past the objections and opened up. I found this out as one of my friends had happened upon it and put up a post on social media that he was at the pub. I have been impressed with how Phil is willing to listen to his customers and source his beer and cider accordingly. I will nearly always find a stout or porter, but even if I don't, there will be others that I can drink. There appears to be a core of local residents that are going in there regularly, keeping his till ticking over. About six weeks into his business going live, the local Molly dancing side decided to do a little stint outside the pub. I wasn't aware of this and had decided to go there to meet a friend. When I arrived, it was bursting at the seams. They couldn't all fit in the pub. Mercifully, it was a perfect weather day that day, so

Phil, the licensee, and his wife had a baptism of fire. They did very well but had to get more beer in for the next week as their stock had been seriously depleted—a delightful problem to have. I am hopeful that this pub will continue doing what it's doing. It is already building up its own identity, which I think is essential to these little places. They need to have something about them that is different from all the rest. The alternative is just a homogenous group of beer houses that is only separated by geography. I want some other reason for going to a micro, something that is unique to that pub. This one is going that way.

Worthing

A little town on the South coast at the end of the A24, the road connecting London to the South coast, sitting somewhere between Brighton and Portsmouth. We went there a few times when we were helping out at Amberley Open-Air Working Museum. It was a short distance from Amberley and meant we did not have to wake up at an ungodly hour to get to the museum by 9 am. It has three micropubs at last count, only two to which we have been – the Georgi Fin and the Green Man. The reason for this is that, inexplicably, they all close at 9 pm every day. This is usually the time that we are going out for the night, so Worthing really doesn't work for us. The Georgi Fin and the Green Man are good pubs with good beer at reasonable prices, and I would go there if they were open when I want to go to a pub. I am aware that in a previous chapter, I stated that Cobbett's closed at nine and that I was happy with this. It has to be noted that Cobbett's is the only pub in town with these hours, while in Worthing, it is all of the micropubs, so there is a difference.

Chichester

A little further down the coast from Worthing, one finds Chichester. I have never felt that this is a town that I could get used to. I can't say why; it's just a feeling. It just isn't one or the other—neither small town nor large Village; neither a seaside resort nor inland town. There were two micropubs that we went to. One was a hipster but themed around bicycles. And the other was the Hornet. I liked the Hornet. It is deceptively large as it has an upstairs area. The beer range was good and varied. I have only been there twice, but if I find myself in Chichester, that is the place I would want to go. As far as atmosphere, this is difficult as we went there when we were easing up on our Covid restrictions. All pubs were struggling at that time, and I would not judge any of them for anything that happened during that period.

A lot of the previous paragraph is in the past tense for a reason. I was there recently on one of my folky outings. The Hornet has changed hands to the owners of a local brewery that the Hornet used regularly – the Little Monster Brewery. Unfortunately, this brewery is only interested in fizz. They have a small and uninteresting range of three cask beers, all pretty much the same. This is a real locals pub, and the older locals still go there, so I suppose they have to cater for them. But they earn much more from mediocre fizz that they don't have to look after so much and can source directly from their own brewery. No middlemen, no transport costs, higher profit margin. (Their own beer is priced the same as the ones from other breweries.) This means that the cask ales tend to take a back seat. They also advertise their closing time as 11 pm when it is, in fact, 9.30 pm. Not very professional.

Oh well. What used to be the second-best pub in Chichester, the Hole in the Wall, is now the best. Pity it has six hand pumps but only uses two or three. Fabulous if you like cider, though. A very good range of that.

The Rake

This is a small pub at the back of Borough Market in the London Bridge area. The Market is a tourist trap and is therefore prohibitively expensive, and this pub is no different. It is a bit hipster, although it does serve a decent cask ale or four. Because of the restrictions during lockdown, they have opened up some areas outside the pub and put up large parasols to protect from the sun and rain. I go there to meet friends and ex-colleagues once or twice a year, but I couldn't afford to go there more often.

Hoppy Place

This pub is within walking distance from my home. I know this because I walked there once. An unremarkable statement, I know, but let me explain. In our wanderings in search of micropubs, we came across this pub in Windsor. We had no real reason for going there, no family, no ties, nothing. The pub is a bit of a hipster pub dealing with kegged beer and one cask, but it had such a friendly atmosphere that I had to forgive them. The owners are interested in serving good quality beer of various styles, and they have a load of cans and bottles to take away as well. The town has a place specially for motorhomes, so we know there is somewhere for us to park up. We therefore go there from time to time. My son has recently moved in with his girlfriend in Maidenhead, a few short miles away, so we now have reason to go there. My wife and I have taken to walking as a good form of exercise, and we plan on a very long walking holiday. We need to get walking fit, so we decided to do one long walk to see how we faired. Windsor is 23 miles (a little shy of 40km), and the walk took us through Richmond Park and Wimbledon Park—so pleasant walking conditions for much of the way. The walk was not entirely without incident, but we did get there in good time. I went straight up to the bar and said, 'This pub is now officially walking distance from my house because we just walked it.'

The owners have now opened another pub in Maidenhead. This one is an entirely different animal. It had more in the way of cask ales, but it was a much younger clientele. There are no soft furnishings, so I couldn't hear myself think in there with every single person's conversation bouncing off the walls and ceiling and straight into my ear. No, thank you, I'll stick to Windsor.

River Ale House

First question, where's the river? Okay, so there is a little stream sloshing by not too far away called the Thames, but it is over a mile away. You are not going to get your feet wet in that river when you step out of the pub. If I see the word river in a pub name, I expect a river. Anyway, a seriously first-world problem which detracts not one iota from the fact that this is a really nice little pub. It was opened by a chap who had been using the premises to produce and sell Lingerie. He clearly got bored of covering ladies' backsides and decided to try to get them to fall on them instead. He was also a Bruce Springsteen fan. The name is a nod to his best-selling album River. It was CAMRA SE London pub of the year for 2022. Not that this accolade is something that I set much stock by.

There is a good range of dark to light, weak to strong beers on all the time. It is clearly, very much a locals' pub even though it is on a major highway, the South Circular Road in South London, about six bus stops from Greenwich. My only criticism the last time I went in there was that the dark beer I had was served way too cold. Cold is for lagers and light beers. But this is just another first-world problem. If you don't want a cold stout, leave it to rest for a while, it will reach room temperature pretty quickly. Then just get your next round in when you are still only halfway down your current beer. It does tend to keep the beer in better condition for longer, so it isn't really a problem. Dog friendly, music friendly, and, most importantly, friendly pub. It is a little off the beaten track for me, so I only really go there when I am working at Greenwich Market. I do this on Wednesdays, so I only ever go into the pub on that day.

I was also intrigued by the type of people who went in there to drink. This pub has all the markings of an 'old geezer's' pub, and yet, we were sitting next to a group of three young American ladies all in their twenties. When they left, they were replaced by various youngish student types who all seemed to know the pub well enough. There was a core of the 'old geezer' element, but young people were there as well. This is a good thing in my book and a definite tick in the box for them.

The Four Candles

The smallest pub in the UK that has its own brewery on the premises. It only seemed to serve its own cask beers, and this comprised a bitter, a pale and an IPA. The pale was a perfectly pleasant beer. It was never going to blow your socks off but pleasant, nevertheless. Pleasingly, they had a display of four Candles right next to another display of Fork Handles. There were other references to the famous Two Ronnies sketch. The walls are filled with cartoon strips from magazines like Private Eye and Readers Digest. It sits directly across the road from The Albion Pub, A traditional pub that serves nothing that I can drink. The customers at the Four Candles are happy with this arrangement as all the youngsters stick to the other pub and leave them in peace.

Northward Ho!

We could stay around the southern part of England indefinitely and never run out of micropubs, but that would not make for good research. Purely in the spirit of doing serious research, and not, as some nay-sayers may suggest, just going out on a jolly, we headed for the frozen wastelands of the North of England. It was, after all, coming to the end of a particularly cold winter, and I had had enough of the frozen wastelands of the south.

The Rusty Barrel, Rugeley, Staffordshire

The first stop was Peterborough, which I describe in a later chapter on traditional pubs. Then onto Rugeley in Staffordshire. This sounds quite random. It is a small town very close to the spot that is the furthest point from the sea anywhere in England – Lichfield. It is not as random as it at first seems. I have tenuous links to the area. We had just been to visit a very good friend in nearby Cannock who has been rendered housebound due to medical issues. I have had relatives living in the town in the past – in fact, they moved to Peterborough, where they still reside. It also has one vital ingredient apropos to this tome – a micropub. The Rusty Barrel is the only one ever to have been licenced in Rugeley and a pub that I found very comfortable. It had all the things that I liked – good conversation, good décor, no loud music, no TV, no fruit machines and a good range of beers at very reasonable prices. It was very much catering to the locals; everyone seemed to know each other by name. It was friendly and welcoming. We have returned to this pub and was pleased to find that much of the people there recognised us from our last visit. As we weren't hoofed out on our ears, we took this to be positive. I will be going to see my friend again, and I will be detouring to this pub when I do.

The Shambles, York, Yorkshire

We now go from small, central England to the somewhat larger tourist city of York. I am not a city person, but I do quite like York. It is not as impersonal as London or Birmingham. It is as, if not more, historic, though. It retains this history as it was not destroyed in the second world war, so it feels old. We didn't see much of the city, because, as much as I do like it, it is still a city and I prefer the open spaces of the countryside. Having done the obligatory Sunday Market and taken in a street entertainer, we repaired to our first micropub, the Shambles. This pub is to be found on the road of that name, a medieval road known for the butcher's trade. Outside the pub will be found a long queue of people waiting to get into a shop that has something to do with the spirit world. I am informed that a social media post went viral, and now everyone wants a piece of the action. If one sidles up the inside of this queue, one will find a pub. It is tiny at the front bar. There is seating for three people and standing room for three or four others. It opens up at the back to a fairly substantial, if impersonal, room that will comfortably seat 20 or more on very well-spaced tables. There is also an enclosed space at the back outside the pub that will seat 20 more.

I was interested in the front room. Although tiny, it was very much a place where you just slot into the conversation or stay silent. I went for option one. Although the pub seemed to be a local's pub, the people who were there, although familiar with the pub, were all from different places. There was someone from Liverpool, a chap from Derby who had just returned from a twenty-year visit to Japan and various other people, none of whom had Yorkshire accents. The beer was of a good standard. I was drinking the dark mild, a drink I usually avoid, and I am not sure why I stayed on it; plenty of other beers are on offer.

We left there to go and feed ourselves and check out another pub called The House of Trembling Madness. This pub only served Kegged beer and was therefore overpriced. It is enormous. It felt like the foyer of a large hotel. The toilets were on the third floor despite there being enough room to land a small aircraft on the ground floor. All the other floors had the same feel to them. No conversation, no atmosphere, no reason to buy a second beer, no reason to return unless you like expensive fizzy beer. So back to the Shambles, it was. A local man-and-guitar had set up and was knocking out competent renditions of popular 70's, 80's and 90's favourites. This was being performed out the back, where the cold temperatures overrode our desire to listen to his music, so we went back inside. This is a good thing, as it meant that one could listen to it if one wanted to and avoid it if one did not. The door to the outside was well insulated, and one could hardly hear it even though he was just the other side of a glass door – until the door was opened to let someone in or out. In fact, one could hear the music better while standing in the large Market place to the rear of the pub than one could from the inside.

Without a single 'ey oop', 'Eee baa gûm' or a hiccough in place of the word 'the' being uttered by anyone, it was time to leave the wilds of Yorkshire for the gentle slopes of the Peak District, where we watched the rain cascading for two days. Hayfield seems like a nice place to visit, but nothing to write about on this subject. So, on to Ludlow.

We like Ludlow. We go there at least once a year. It is food central for the UK and has a food festival every year. It also went viral, and now everyone wants a piece of the action. If one sidles up the inside of this queue, one will find a pub. It is tiny at the front bar. There is seating for three people and standing room for three or four others. It opens up at the back to a fairly substantial, if impersonal, room that will comfortably seat 20 or more on very well-spaced tables. There is also an enclosed space at the back outside the pub that will seat 20 more.

I was interested in the front room. Although tiny, it was very much a place where you just slot into the conversation or stay silent. I went for option one. Although the pub seemed to be a local's pub, the people who were there, although familiar with the pub, were all from different places. There was someone from Liverpool, a chap from Derby who had just returned from a twenty-year visit to Japan and various other people, none of whom had Yorkshire accents. The beer was of a good standard. I was drinking the dark mild, a drink I usually avoid, and I am not sure why I stayed on it; plenty of other beers are on offer.

We left there to go and feed ourselves and check out another pub called The House of Trembling Madness. This pub only served Kegged beer and was therefore overpriced. It is enormous. It felt like the foyer of a large hotel. The toilets were on the third floor despite there being enough room to land a small aircraft on the ground floor. All the other floors had the same feel to them. No conversation, no atmosphere, no reason to buy a second beer, no reason to return unless you like expensive fizzy beer. So back to the Shambles, it was. A local man-and-guitar had set up and was knocking out competent renditions of popular 70's, 80's and 90's favourites. This was being performed out the back, where the cold temperatures overrode our desire to listen to his music, so we went back inside. This is a good thing, as it meant that one could listen to it if one wanted to and avoid it if one did not. The door to the outside was well insulated, and one could hardly hear it even though he was just the other side of a glass door – until the door was opened to let someone in or out. In fact, one could hear the music better while standing in the large Market place to the rear of the pub than one could from the inside.

Without a single 'ey oop', 'Eee baa gûm' or a hiccough in place of the word 'the' being uttered by anyone, it was time to leave the wilds of Yorkshire for the gentle slopes of the Peak District, where we watched the rain cascading for two days. Hayfield seems like a nice place to visit, but nothing to write about on this subject. So, on to Ludlow.

We like Ludlow. We go there at least once a year. It is food central for the UK and has a food festival every year. It also has rather expensive food halls just outside the town. I could spend a lot of money there. The food is locally produced and, without the strictures placed on them by multicorporate nasties, sell very high-quality produce. Our main issue is that whenever we have gone to Ludlow, it has been a Tuesday. This seems to be the day when everyone in the entire town just doesn't bother to get out of bed. Micro pubs are always closed and, apart from the Brewery Tap, which closes at 5.30 pm every day, the pub scene is nothing to write home about. So we have seldom been able to pay visits to the bastions of the industry. This time, we decided to avoid Tuesday – hence the two-day layup in Hayfield.

Old Street Tavern and the Blood Bay, Ludlow, Shropshire

The Old Street Tavern is one pub that we did manage to visit many years ago and have wanted to return ever since. It was a tiny place on the first floor of a terraced row close to the town centre. It was run by a South African Chap passionate about his little project. On our return, it had changed somewhat. There were new tenants running the place. They had also taken the ground floor, transforming the pub from a tiny Micro to a very small one. The atmosphere was great, the conversation flowed, and the beer was good. Unfortunately, it was also strong, which didn't work out well for me. This was the first and only occasion on this entire trip where I over-indulged spectacularly. The beer of choice was Abduction – a rather strong pale ale – and it abducted my common sense.

I can't blame it all on the Old Street Tavern. We did feel the need to visit the other micro in town with the slightly worrying name of The Blood Bay. Not being a very horsey-type-person, I had to be told that this referenced a racehorse breed. Again. This is a very small micro close to the open-air marketplace that appears to only open on days we are not there. We were served by a bright, intelligent young Irish lady who joined our conversations and wasn't afraid to stray into the murky pub taboos of politics and religion.

All in all, a pleasant interlude with good beer and company. We did, however, feel the need to return to the Old Street tavern as I had not yet worked out that I had probably had enough. I had finally sussed it all out the following day when I felt like I had been run over by a bus.

The rest of our journey did not uncover any new micros. We dropped into our friends in Ross-on-Wye as a surprise. The welcome was, as expected, warm and genuine, and the beer was top-notch. He is now brewing his own product full-time and looking to sell to other local pubs, so it is all looking good for him. We then went through that mecca of common sense and temperance that calls itself Glastonbury. As ever, common sense and temperance were well disguised, so we decided to take the lead and book into a proper campsite to avail ourselves of a decent shower. We had heard about a pub in Pulborough, so we investigated the next day, intending to be in that area anyway. They seem to close down anything remotely similar to a decent pub, so we placed Pulborough firmly in our rear-view mirror and headed for nearby Arundel – which does not seem to have the same attitude to pubs.

Stratford Alehouse

As I am going through the process of publishing, I am constantly finding new places. Some are ok and not really worthy of making the changes, but some are well worth a mention. We were out and about in Staffordshire and Warwickshire this last week meeting friends and checking out pubs. Stratford-on-Avon lives and dies by it's link to the Bard and as such has little else to offer. For those who like to quaff a beer or two, it's a bit of a desert. The Stratford Alehouse bucks this trend. The only micropub in town and does everything I want in a pub of this sort. The landlord says he was number 63 on the micropub list – this being a chronological record of these establishments. He has been going for 10 years and knows all his customers.

He doesn't attract tourists, so it is all local trade. Good range of beer, good conversation. Good feel.

Tamworth Brewing Co, Staffordshire

Is this a Micro? It's a big one, it has a ground floor, first floor and second floor. If my definition is anything to go by, it has to be a micro pub with brewery attached as it does not have a history within the pub industry. It started off as a brewery in a single terraced premises. They expanded when they bought the next door premises and moved the brewery to the new purchase while opening a pub on the old site. They then expanded again by buying another adjoining premises. It hasn't looked back since. It is a pub that has live music, jam sessions, board games, beer, beer and more beer at reasonable prices and always in good condition. Good conversations and an easy-going atmosphere on any day of the week and any time of the day. Although I am a little cool about CAMRA accolades, it has to be doing well if it has become the best pub in Great Britain two years running. Or is it simply the fact that the CAMRA members who go there are more vocal than everyone else. It is a great pub and wild horses wouldn't drag me away if I happen to be in the area...but better than every other pub? I am aware that they take all sorts of different criteria into account when they make these decisions, but still a very subjective judgement I would suggest. I know I would struggle to put my finger on the best pub that I have been to, they all have different qualities that make them unique. But a great pub for all that and well worth a visit.

Traditional Pubs

For balance, I feel I have to look at the traditional pubs. Although I have not exactly flown their flags thus far, I am the first to admit that there are enough good-quality traditional pubs out there. They are, for the most part, free houses, and those that aren't are owned by smaller enterprises.

The Hope

This is what I would call my local. Anyone who frequents pubs will have a favourite close to where they live. They would probably be well-known as regular customers and have friends that go there as well. The Hope is the first pub in London owned wholly by members of the local community. Now at this point, I need to point out that this accolade is actually claimed by another, The Ivy House. This is a good pub that is, indeed, community-owned. It is also in London, so most of what they say is true. The issue is that the Hope was founded in 2010, and the Ivy House was founded in 2013. Unless my arithmetic is completely out, the Hope predates them by three years. If it is the location they are at issue with, and the argument I have heard is that the Hope isn't in London. Well, that can be dealt with easily enough. Their local taxes go to the London Mayor; London's Met police cover the area;

London Ambulance service covers the area, and the London Fire Brigade does so as well. Enough said.

Up to 2010, The Hope was a rough pub owned by a pub co. Because of what was happening, the local community made moves to have its license revoked. A group of local people put their collective heads together and managed to buy a twenty-year 'free of tie' lease. How they managed a free-of-tie lease is the subject of conjecture. They would say that their outstanding negotiating skill came to the fore. One of the founder members, however, told me that the Pub co was notorious for not paying their suppliers, despite insisting that their pubs be prompt with their accounts. It got to the point where the suppliers cut the company off, and they were forced to write to all their pubs and allow them to trade off-tie while they sorted their accounts out.

Unfortunately for them, they neglected to put an end-by date to this instruction. As a result, The Hope started sourcing from local microbreweries and continued after the pub co had sorted its issues out. After some time, the pub co realised that they hadn't been supplying the Hope and made contact. The Hope responded by saying that they had a letter allowing them to trade off-tie. "Ah," said the rep, "that was only supposed to be until we sorted our issues out". "Not according to this letter written by you. It clearly stated that we can trade off-tie. It doesn't say anything about time limits". "Well, you must continue trading through us". "No." "If you don't, we will take you to court." "Crack on, we still have this letter, and it is clearly telling us to trade off-tie." The pub co eventually relented, and they never went back. In fact, they sold the freehold after about five or so years and broke all ties. I don't know what the truth is, but this sounds feasible, and even if it isn't true, I like the story.

I first went in there knowing none of this. I had hardly ever been to Carshalton for any extended period, and so knew none of the protagonists. My wife and I walk in there to find a range of decent beer on rather rickety hand pumps. The beer garden was uninhabitable. We sat at the front near the window and were, in due course, approached by a bearded 60-something chap with an oversized tankard. He started talking to us about the pub and what they intended to do with the place. He was one of the founder members and called himself Rodger. I don't really know, but I think he was keen to ensure that we were the sort of people that they would have in his pub. In other words, he was vetting us. Having established our 'pv', he was keen to let us know how they were going to proceed. I didn't believe for a moment that they would achieve half of their grandiose plans, but they were good plans, and if they only achieved half, it would be a good thing. They had a seven-year plan to sort everything out and make the pub a shining light that all other pubs should follow. In the end, they had all but achieved everything they had set out to do within five years. They did this having never gone into the red, never borrowed any money and never made a day-on-day loss at the bar. It was by far and away the most popular pub within a five-mile radius. They got rid of all the usual lagers and Guinness and replaced them with seven hand pumps for beer. They always had two dark beers, an IPA, a pale ale and a bitter, all of which were ever-changing, along with two mid-range light ales that were permanent features. Continental beers replaced the lagers. There were Key-kegged ales and real ciders on all the time. No TV, no fruit machines, no Pool Tables — although there was a bar billiards table that was so old it only took florins — and no jukebox, although there was a guitar, ukelele and a piano if you wanted to make your own music. They now have ten beer festivals a year, folk jam sessions every week, Mensa meetings, fly-tying nights, and a load more stuff. They even had music festivals for a couple of years. I had my retirement party there, where I was allowed five different folks bands, catering for all my guests and was even allowed to bring a cask of ale that was gifted to me.

What I find fascinating about the place is the customers. This is on the outskirts of one of the world's best-known cities on the planet. London is a huge, busy, diverse place with a largely international, transient population amongst a large number of local Londoners. It is not unusual to find people who have friends they have known their whole lives, but it is unusual to find an entire town full of them. And yet this pub seems to attract people who are in their 50s and 60s and seem to have all known each other throughout their entire lives. It isn't like rural Cornwall, where everyone is born in the same hospital, goes to the same school, works in the same pubs as school leavers, gets jobs and marries all within the same area. These are people who get to their fifties and have little or no conversation outside local gossip. At the Hope, they seem to have done all the first bits – born in the same hospital etc. But they have then left and found a life elsewhere, married elsewhere, and got jobs elsewhere. Then they all came back full of life experiences and interesting conversations. It feels almost incestuous, but it isn't.

I have had the privilege to watch this pub grow from humble beginnings to achieve all its ambitions. It shrugged off lockdown by completing renovations ahead of schedule so that when we came back, we had an improved environment. Good pub

The Trafalgar

Although this is a traditional pub, it is smaller than your average micro. It is the oldest free house in Merton, apparently, and is effectively the sister pub to the Hope. It can be found in an ugly little housing estate that backs onto South Wimbledon Underground Station. It is small enough that one can sit at one end of the 'lounge' and have a reasonable conversation with only slightly raised voices, with another person sitting on the far side of the bar. It was no more than three metres wide at its widest. This is a small pub.

When I first went in there, it was run by Dave Norman. It was clearly a local's pub, as there was no passing trade of any description. The locals were, however, friendly, and the beer was OK. Dave liked live music and appeared to have a lot of contacts in this area, so we were privileged to meet some fine musicians. We had a jazz afternoon on Sundays, where I met Mike and Ruth and have become firm friends. We met the recently departed Tony Coe – a jazz sax player well-known in jazz circles. One chap, Steve Whalley, who came to play a blues set, was a man who had played with some of the greats like Ry Cooder, Slade and Chuck Berry – who he called the boss among others. He came into the pub and walked up to the bar staff. He politely introduced himself as the musician for the night and asked to be shown to the main bar. "where you are standing is the main bar, and where you have just walked through is the lounge bar where you will be playing." I know this story is true because this is what he told us during his set. He was a consummate professional who looked at the bedraggled, crusty old council estate geezers and started playing. Within 10 minutes, he had them all eating out of his hand. He had three instruments, an electric guitar, a semi-acoustic guitar and a mandolin. They were all Fender and all given to him in payment for one gig. That is £1000 worth of kit there for two hours work. But he was worth it. He then stood there and heaped praise on the pub and begged people to keep places like that alive as they were the bedrock of this nation.

Given the size of the pub, it always amused me that one guy who used to pop in fairly infrequently stood 7'02" in his socks. He was no weed, either. This guy was enormous, loud and strong, and so incongruous, but we all genuinely liked him sitting there playing dominoes with his mate.

This pub continued like this for a while until one day, we were in there listening to our Sunday afternoon jazz and talking about who would be there next week when my wife overheard a conversation to the effect that the pub was closing and would not be there the following Sunday. This was news to the band, who simply hadn't been told. I think Dave got the hell in and made the decision, then told the landlord to shove it all where the sun don't shine that day and just hadn't got around to telling anyone.

My wife and I accompanied Mike and Ruth to the Hope, full of the hot-off-the-press news. I noticed a little gleam in Rodger's eye, but nothing further was said until five days later when he sidled up to me and told me not to worry about the Traf.

True to his word, he had obtained the lease, and within a couple of weeks, he had renovated it and reopened it. The beer range was vastly improved, but inexplicably, he had told the darts team that they would have to find somewhere else. The cricket team went the same way as did the Sunday jazz. Now these were all drinking people. This was a strange decision in a pub with no passing trade. He did entice the cricket team back but not the darts or jazz. He told me that too many people were complaining about the jazz, so he had to get rid of it. What he didn't understand was that Sundays comprised three types of people. The musicians, who drank his beer, but not much (between five and seven people). The people who went there week on week to watch the jazz and who drank beer (Between eight and twelve people); and the people who went there week on week to drink beer and complain about the jazz and who drank lots of beer (Around eight to ten people). When the jazz went, so did the audience, and so did the complainers. They just went to find some other pub to drink and complain. So a pub that really did need all the custom they could get, shooed away between 20 and 30 people a week in one stroke. Rodger won't admit this now, but that was not his greatest hour. In the end, the customers made that pub, half of whom were musicians. I used to like going in there because there was always someone in there I could sit and chat with or maybe have an impromptu jam.

Rodger did keep the other music going and started a folk jam session on Wednesdays (or at least got someone else to start one). The beer was always good, so I continued going there. In 2022, the council descended on the pub and shut it down because the building wasn't fit for purpose. I suspect that it was because there was a lot of regeneration going on in the estate, and they wanted the land. I don't know the full story, and I suspect I won't find the whole truth, but the council were not able to renovate, and the pub is due to reopen in the late summer of 2023. I'll watch this space.

The Sultan, South Wimbledon

Ten minute's walk from the Traf in a quiet residential street in South Wimbledon; one will find the Sultan Arms. This is a tied pub! Whatever next. It is owned by Hop Back

Brewery, which is based in Swindon. This is a relatively small brewery that brews a good range of light, dark, strong and weak beers. I believe the owner hails from Wimbledon and wanted a pub in the area in which he grew up.

Most of his pubs seem to be dotted around the area between Swindon and the south coast, and they all have a similar feel. Same sturdy-looking pine tables and chairs. Same light-coloured décor. Same beer range. It is sort of comforting to know what a pub is going to be like before you even walk in there.

The Sultan is an odd one. I want to like the pub. There are all the things I like about the pub, and it is a reasonable distance away. I have never had any trouble in there. I still can't put my finger on it, but I never feel comfortable in there and am always wondering what pub we are going to go to next. It tends to go through managers a lot. This is never good. I am of the school of thought that people seldom leave bad jobs; they leave bad managers. I couldn't say whether the Hop Back Brewery is a good or bad employer. They do go through them, so I am left wondering. The problem is that each manager wants to put his or her stamp on the pub, so it keeps changing. Some have the full beer range on all the time, and some only put the two most popular. Some want all sorts of different events, and some don't.

Currently, it is run by someone who may be teetotal or at least not a big drinker. This is odd for a pub that relies on the staff looking after the beer and knowing when it is in good condition. Having said that, he has the full range on all the time, and I haven't had a bad pint in there. It is a cashless pub. I don't particularly like that. I prefer the choice. I get that some small pubs went cash-free when they kept getting robbed. That makes sense. The Sultan is in an area that is not blighted by this sort of thing, and I have never heard of them or any other local pub having this sort of problem, so I would prefer it if they gave me the choice. A minor issue, but these little gripes mount up.

The pub itself lives in a quiet residential street only a couple hundred yards from the main high street. It has no passing trade. One would only go there if one knew it was there. This being said, I don't get the impression that the local residents use it that much. I am told that they are constantly objecting to noise and disturbances outside the pub. I thought this strange as I had never witnessed any of those sorts of issues. I then learned that the complainants didn't live anywhere near the pub but were from a religious sect that doesn't like alcohol. I wonder if I made spurious complaints about the religious sect, would the council shut them down?

The pub is split in two, and one can only get between them by either going through the toilets or going outside and coming back in through a separate entrance. The one side is small and comfortable and tends to be used by musicians having jam sessions in there or darts people. The other larger part is where most people go and opens out onto a small uninteresting beer garden. This is a good arrangement as those who aren't interested in music, darts or whatever else is happening there can simply walk through to the other bit and ignore it.

In conclusion, I am not a big fan of this pub, but I can offer no real reason. This can only mean that it is a good pub, and it is just me being me. Try it out, don't take my word for it.

Kraft Pub and Kitchen

Now this was a revelation in the pub experience. The guys that run this pub started with a place halfway between Victoria and Pimlico in Central London. It was a small place with no soft furnishings and probably insulated to within an inch of its life. It meant that there was nowhere for sound to escape. If there was more than one group of people, it was a cacophony of noise. If they were playing music, you could hear the drum beat and maybe a little bass, but nothing else over the din.

This being said, it was an ambitious pub. It was in a premises that had no previous pub history, so, by my own definition, a micropub. It boasted a dozen hand pumps for cask ale and a bewildering array of kegged ales and continental lagers. I had never seen so many beers in a pub before – every style and strength you wanted. They were on a mission to promote decent beer and reasonable prices. I was all for this. It was, unsurprisingly, a success. So much so that before long, another one appeared in Farringdon, then Clapham and Brixton. He even opened one in Brighton. Some of these were on traditional pub premises, and some, like his first one, were in alternative venues. I did have an issue with the one in Farringdon that I felt I had to point out to the owners. This was a large place with two storeys and one long straight flight of stairs with a clear Perspex balustrade between the two floors. This meant that if you looked up to the top of the stairs while standing to the side of the flight, young ladies dressed in their skimpiest finery were showing more than they realised. Once you've seen it, you can't unsee it, so I pointed this out. I spent the rest of the evening looking no higher than eye level, just in case. Whether he rectified the problem or just strategically positioned himself and his spurious complaints about the religious sect, would the council shut them down?

The pub is split in two, and one can only get between them by either going through the toilets or going outside and coming back in through a separate entrance. The one side is small and comfortable and tends to be used by musicians having jam sessions in there or darts people. The other larger part is where most people go and opens out onto a small uninteresting beer garden. This is a good arrangement as those who aren't interested in music, darts or whatever else is happening there can simply walk through to the other bit and ignore it.

In conclusion, I am not a big fan of this pub, but I can offer no real reason. This can only mean that it is a good pub, and it is just me being me. Try it out, don't take my word for it.

Kraft Pub and Kitchen

Now this was a revelation in the pub experience. The guys that run this pub started with a place halfway between Victoria and Pimlico in Central London. It was a small place with no soft furnishings and probably insulated to within an inch of its life. It meant that there was nowhere for sound to escape. If there was more than one group of people, it was a cacophony of noise. If they were playing music, you could hear the drum beat and maybe a little bass, but nothing else over the din.

This being said, it was an ambitious pub. It was in a premises that had no previous pub history, so, by my own definition, a micropub. It boasted a dozen hand pumps for cask ale and a bewildering array of kegged ales and continental lagers. I had never seen so many beers in a pub before – every style and strength you wanted. They were on a mission to promote decent beer and reasonable prices. I was all for this. It was, unsurprisingly, a success. So much so that before long, another one appeared in Farringdon, then Clapham and Brixton. He even opened one in Brighton. Some of these were on traditional pub premises, and some, like his first one, were in alternative venues. I did have an issue with the one in Farringdon that I felt I had to point out to the owners. This was a large place with two storeys and one long straight flight of stairs with a clear Perspex balustrade between the two floors. This meant that if you looked up to the top of the stairs while standing to the side of the flight, young ladies dressed in their skimpiest finery were showing more than they realised. Once you've seen it, you can't unsee it, so I pointed this out. I spent the rest of the evening looking no higher than eye level, just in case. Whether he rectified the problem or just strategically positioned himself and his mates, I don't know. I haven't been back there since. Not because of this, it is just a little off the beaten track for me.

I am aware that this chain of pubs is still doing well. I think that some have closed, and new ones opened up. I believe this model has been taken seriously, and new pubs are seriously considering the range of beer they put on—such a far cry from the less-than-halcyon days of the 60s and 70s. My only criticism would be that each and every one of the outlets that I have been into has felt a little too impersonal for my tastes. This entry goes under the' traditional' heading because some are and some aren't, but all have that corporate feel. A landlord is there to sell alcohol to people for consumption on the premises. That is fine, but it isn't the only reason customers go in there. If all I wanted to do were drink beer, I'd go to the supermarket and buy a load at half the price of pub beers and sit at home gazing unblinkingly at the television and descending into oblivion. That is not me, and I want something more out of a pub.

Bricklayer Putney

Is this a good pub? Well it depends on when you ask. Ten years ago, it was a good pub that had elements that I didn't like. Five years ago, I wouldn't go in there. Last year it had returned with knobs on. Let me explain.

This is a pub that is nestled in a side street off the Lower Richmond Road, which runs alongside the Thames River in Putney. Were it not for very tall buildings in rather inconvenient locations, it would be a hundred or so yards from Putney High Street. As it is, you are at least three hundred yards because of the circuitous route you have to take. It sits right at the end of a cul-de-sac so that you can see it from the main road, but it is a little too far for it to have 'passing Trade'. The pub was bequeathed to a woman and, it was expected, would be sold on to some corporate redevelopment company. In the event, she decided to take it on and built up a relationship with the Timothy Taylor Brewery. Although it is a genuine free house, it always had a range of their beers. It gathered together a few awards through CAMRA, although this was tainted by the fact that the Local CAMRA group would use that pub as a meeting place. So they would always put their favourite pub up for awards even when it wasn't doing so well. As a result of this, South West London CAMRA changed its policy so that no pub could win an award two years in a row. This made no sense at all. It meant that the recipient of a 'best pub' prize would not necessarily be the best because the best one for that year was disqualified for being too good. Anyway, I could bang

121

on about the inconsistencies of CAMRA 'til the cows come home. This is not the platform for that.

The pub trundled along like that for several years. It had a few beer festivals where they were charging people to use their glasses. This put me off, and I stopped going for a year or so. I then found myself in Putney on the occasion of a London 100-mile cycling event, so we decided to pop in. Given that Putney was packed out – and this was entirely expected – one would have thought that the pubs would surely have stocked up their cellars. We walked in about 10 minutes after they opened. They had two hand pumps working, one of them managed one pint before it was emptied, and the other was not empty because no one wanted to drink it. They had no lager, no Guinness and only white wine. We were told that they had a particularly busy night the night before. No pub will run out of beer after one session. There was clearly an issue. It seemed that the owner was wearying of the pub trade and had taken her eye off the ball. I stopped going altogether.

That is until two years ago when I went in there on the occasion of the Oxford/Cambridge annual boat race. They had put in more hand pumps. They had a much more comprehensive range of beers and ciders. The staff were vibrant and interested, and a sea-change had occurred. I believe that the owner took on a manager to oversee the pub, and he had turned it around. It was nice to see the old pub back bigger and better.

Oaka

I am going to talk about this pub despite the fact that it no longer serves the sort of product that I want because it may come back to what it was. The Oaka in Mansion House Kennington is, or was, owned by Oakham Brewery in Peterborough. It is an odd sort of place. It has the feel of a bar rather than a pub and has a Thai restaurant attached. This means that half of it is a fully-fledged restaurant with everything you'd expect of a restaurant, while the other half is a full-time pub serving all the Oakham cask range alongside some kegged lagers and ales. One can eat in the pub area and drink in the restaurant area, even though they are pretty distinct from each other. It is quite close to central London, so the prices are a little uppish, but one would expect that. The staff were always friendly and pampered our dog when we took him there. Whenever we turned up without the dog, they demanded to know where he was. It was a pub I always felt very comfortable in. Here is the problem. I would go there at eight in the evening on a Friday, and it was almost empty. I don't know what the daytime trade was like, but pubs live for Friday and Saturday nights. If they are quiet, then you have problems. I think the brewery wanted a foothold in London, and this was it. They were prepared to take the hit for one premises. Ultimately, it was not sustainable, and the last time I went in there, they had removed all the cask ales and were only selling lagers. It was even quieter than normal, and we did not increase their numbers.

The thing is that they do have a brewery tap in Peterborough. This is the same as the Oaka in Kennington, only four times bigger. In a previous chapter called 'Northward Ho!' where I described a trip to the north of England, our first stop was this very pub. To say I was conflicted when I left is understating it. We walked in to find a good range of Oakham beers, some guest beers and everything one would expect. We went to sit down and commented on the rather ample empty space in front of the bar. It seemed incongruous for a pub like this. We then noticed that a DJ would be descending on the place at around 9.30 pm. Not what we were hoping for. We had eaten and were settling down to a few beers before bedtime. 9.30 pm crept up on us, and before we knew what was happening, the pub – that had hitherto been inhabited by crusty old geezers drinking cask ale – had transformed into a fully functioning nightclub. Scantily clad youngsters drinking shots from a tray that was being walked around by scantily clad bar staff was the order of the day. No one took a blind bit of notice to us when we bought one more pint of Oakham Citra, sat and drank it in a state of bemusement, and then left for bed.

This is not a tale of woe. It is a pub that is seeing business opportunities with the young and the old. I saw adverts for jazz nights and open mic nights. There were all sorts of events covering the whole gamut. I think this was a good thing. Nightclubs, at my stage of life, I can do without, but hats off to them—pity about the Oaka in Kennington.

Chequers Inn, Little Gransden

Now we find ourselves in a tiny Cambridgeshire village with a total of six roads and one pub. But what a pub. We have just been roaming around the southern half of the UK, discovering different pubs and were on our final stretch. We decided that a campsite just outside of Great Gransden (ten roads, so huge by comparison) would be good as it would be a short final leg. This is the far Southwest of the county and not that far from the northern stretch of the M25. The campsite owner told us that the pub in the village wasn't great and didn't allow dogs, but that the next town along, Little Gransden had what we were looking for. We confirmed that the first pub wasn't going to work for us and walked the extra mile or so to the next village. This is a small pub. It was taken on by an ex-RAF pilot after the end of the second world war.

It remains in the same family's hands, although they struggle to get their offspring interested enough to take it on when they retire. It had a dining area that was exclusively for dining, so the pub was compact. Good for me because we got to communicate. They had a decent selection of beer on, one of which was a dark mild. I don't normally go for this type of beer, it is usually weak in strength and flavour and lacking in body and always seems like something of an afterthought. Being the only dark beer on, I was compelled to try it out. It was the best beer I had sampled in the last two weeks. It was full of flavour, slightly higher than average abv and had body. I stayed on that for the evening and kept to it the second time around a few months later. I am told that they brew the beer on the premises and sell it on the premises and nowhere else. As an aside, while chatting to the owner, we found that he had been to our local, the Traf. It's weird how such a little pub can have seen people from so far and wide visiting it. It's also weird how we keep finding them.

The King Arthur, Glastonbury

We now return to that mecca of common-sense and temperance that calls itself Glastonbury. Stephen Fry is famously from Norfolk. I heard him talking about humorous abbreviations, one of which was something a that a doctor used in his notes. For those who are not aware of the history, Norfolk has a reputation for inbreeding. I don't know where it comes from and I am sure that in this day and age, it is entirely unjustified. But it is the subject of ribaldry among the comedy circuit. The abbreviation, 'NFN' apparently meant 'Normal for Norfolk', and I take it that this was meant in a medical sense. The guy had obviously never been to Glastonbury. Then again, nothing is 'normal' there. I get the impression that pubs aren't a big draw for visitors. They seem to be a little more spiritual and tend towards other forms of socialising. It was therefore a surprise that we found The King Arthur. Another pub that we happened into while the UK were still struggling to wrench itself out of the COVID pandemic. Pubs were open by now and normality was returning but only very slowly. We wandered in to find some decent looking beers on at the hand pump and ordered a pint each. It's a big pub with lots of different sections and a big beer garden. Difficult to gauge the atmosphere as it was unusual circumstances. We start chatting to the chap behind the bar as he was the only person there. By the end of our pint we had struck up a good wide-ranging conversation and ordered a second. We also offered the barman – who, it turned out, ran the pub – a drink. 'Thanks, but I don't drink alcohol,' he said politely declining. This is unusual to say the least. Cask ale needs care and attention, and the staff need to know that the beer is in good condition. One can only know this if one tastes it. It transpired that he employed a cellar man who was on top of this so all was well in the King Arthur – unusual, but well. In the meantime, another chap, who had come in and was sitting at the bar started chatting. He was cock-a-hoop as he had just opened a fish and chip restaurant in Clevedon, about 15 miles down the road at the mouth of the Severn estuary. During the course of the conversation, it turned out that he didn't know the quality of his product either as he was vegan. So now we have a tee-total pub manager and a vegan fish and chip shop owner in Glastonbury. Very much a case of NFG, I think. We have been back there in busier times. A little different as the had live music going on somewhere within the pub. Not quite our taste from the clientele that were coming and going.

George and Dragon, Chacombe, Northants

Now here's a story to conjure with. A 'small world' story that will be hard to better in terms of time and distance. Modern social media allows us to maintain contact with all manner of people. One such person is a lady who attended the same junior school as I in Harare in the early '70s. She is clearly someone who has taken an interest in the people with whom she grew up. She now lives in New Zealand and I haven't clapped eyes on her for near enough 50 years. She contacted me some time ago and asked how my life had gone and we had a short conversation. She has obviously seen some of my posts and asked if I had heard of the George and Dragon in Chacombe. I had heard of neither the town nor the pub. It is run by a chap who went to my High school in Harare and people seemed to love the pub. I wasn't overly excited about the pub given that Zimbabwe is not exactly a mecca for real ale, but I was intrigued about this chap and thought it would be fun to drop in.

Chacombe is a tiny village comprising about a dozen roads in total on the border between Oxfordshire and Northamptonshire in the midlands in England. This is not normally a good sign as little village pubs have to cater for passing trade and families and normally concentrate on food over beer. We went in anyway and was pleasantly surprised that they had a good range of beer on. We sat down and readied ourselves for an evening of it.

In the event, the man I was hoping to meet was not on duty, but the duty manager came up to us as the result of our enquiries. So there I am sitting in a great pub in a tiny village a hundred miles from my home and five thousand miles from where I spent my formative years – a country I haven't been to since 1985 – and eleven thousand miles from the person who recommended the place. I am talking to a thirty-something Englishman dressed in shorts and flip flops in January and we are talking about people of his acquaintance who were my schoolteachers in Harare forty-five years ago. I remember most teachers from that school but not all, and the two that would immediately come to mind were the two about whom we were talking. They were both alive and well and living local to the pub.

Mini Beer Tour

Throughout the previous pages, I have, from time to time, mentioned mini beer tours. The first of these was in June of 2019. My wife and I had decided to visit some of the pubs that we thought stood out from the crowd. We drew up a list that started at the Radius Arms in Whyteleafe, then went to Margate via Lewes, from where we slowly made our way across the southern counties of England, then briefly into Wales before making our way back through Shropshire to Cambridgeshire. I posted a daily log of our travels on Facebook for posterity starting on day two. I have edited the passages to expand, clarify or correct typos, of which there were plenty, as I always forget to proofread my posts. There are plenty of references to pubs that I have already covered. I make no apologies, although I have not laboured the points too much. Given that the tour was before Covid hit and this is being written in 2023, there have been changes. It is sometimes good to compare thoughts from several years previous to see how they stack up.

23/6/19

Day 2. What can one say about Lewes? This day differed from what we intended to do on this odyssey as we have never been to Lewes, so we didn't know the pubs. The best pub by a distance is the Gardeners arms—small, cosy, good range of beers and knowledgeable staff. Someone wanted to take a half pint away and asked for a plastic mug. They didn't have any. This is a good thing! Beer shouldn't be served in plastic.

On to Margate – or more precisely, Westgate and the Bake and Ale micro. Always very good. The sign outside says open hours are '3 to 9ish'. I love that: plan for a no-plan scenario. We will mooch around Margate for the start of day three, then on to Herne village and the Butchers Arms. Tiny pub complete with a taciturn landlord and good beers.

Day 3. Looks like a change of schedule. We arrived in Herne village at about 4 pm and were concerned to see that there were no opening hours for Sunday at the Butchers Micro (they claim this as the first micro pub in the UK. It was actually open at the time, so obviously, he likes to keep options open for Sunday. We dropped in for a pint to find he was about to call last orders. So what to do with the rest of the day? Quick pint or two of Uber to consider options. We decided to go to Rye a day early and to the Waterworks micro. This is a real go-to pub. If you like beer or cider, this is head and shoulders above anything in Rye. So now it's off to Dorking. I need to replace the water pump in the RV. That is just outside

Guildford, so we will have to be dragged kicking and screaming into Cobbets in Dorking for refreshments. It's a chore, but someone has to do it.

Day 4. Cobbetts in Dorking. For the uninitiated, this is a place that started life as an off-license. They started selling cask-conditioned ale to take away. This became so popular that, after a suggestion from a friend, they obtained an 'on licence' utilising a small room at the back that seats 9 with four standing and similar numbers in the rather grandiosely named 'beer garden'. There are no TVs, fruit machines, or distractions, just beer and conversation. It has since evolved from an off-license with a pub license to a pub with an off-license.

Interesting conversation about a landlord of the Hand in Hand in Wimbledon Common before it was even a twinkle in Young's eye. A landlord who didn't like beer or beer drinkers. He would close the pub at the drop of a hat. If you were banned for any kind of minor breach, you were banned for life. Apparently, even Oliver Reed behaved himself in there, and there are enough stories coming out of the Crooked Billet next door to know that he wasn't in the habit of behaving. This landlord was also generous to a fault when the feeling took him but tight as a duck's anus any other time. He sounds like a proper character, this landlord.

Day 5 takes us to the wilds of the new forest, Hampshire. More specifically, the Cuckoo Inn in Hamptsworth. Hands down the best pub in the new forest. This pub changed hands about six months ago. The manager at the time was doing an excellent job and made a bid for it so that he could continue. He was outbid. I spoke to the new licensee just after he took over. His attitude was – and I quote – 'It ain't broke, so I ain't going to fix it'. Finally, someone with common sense. I am happy to report he was as good as his word. Good beer and good conversation. Great pub. There is an old codger called Jonesy who is in there every day. He is 80+ and more than part of the furniture. I think when he pops his clogs, the building will disintegrate. I did a caricature of him and gave it to the pub. They loved it, but he didn't want it displayed in the pub, so they hung it in the ladies where he won't see it. When he does finally meet his maker, they will mount it over 'his' chair in the pub as a memorial.

Day 6. Another alteration to our highly disciplined schedule. We went into Swanage to visit a premises with an identity crisis. I don't know which came first, but it is a small place that is a butcher, fishmonger, deli, cafe/restaurant, and bar. It only does bottled beers but has a decent selection.

From there, it was onto Draycott, two miles outside Cheddar and The Cider Barn. This is very much the go-to pub for the locals. Though this is hard to confirm because they treat everyone as if they are regulars. They have a bewildering range of ciders, three lagers and two well-kept ales. Normally a bitter and a pale. I am told the food is good pub grub fare. One of the customers asked for a spoon instead of a knife and fork with which to eat his Ruby Murray. The barman presented him with a ladle which he gracefully accepted, and then using said ladle, slightly less than gracefully ate his grub.

Waking up to a cloudless sky with Devon on our to-do list but not before buying some overpriced cheddar from . . . Cheddar?

Day 7. We gave our livers a well-deserved rest. We headed straight to Devon, where there is a campsite with a brewery and pub attached. This is Art Brew, a well-respected brewery that has downsized to a 2.5-barrel brewery in rural Devon and supplies the local pubs. The pub is open only Fridays and Saturdays, so we had a day of rest. I did, of course, have two bottles stashed from our Lewes visit. I was told to try out Harvey's porter. I have no real time for anything Harvey's does. They have been going for 250 years and haven't changed a thing, while everyone else is. Having said that, the porter was very pleasant. Full of flavour and everything that Harvey's isn't used to. If they continue in this direction, I'm going to have to review my opinions. In the meantime, I look forward to a sesh at ArtBrew on the morrow.

Day 8. Livers now Rested, sort of, we stumbled to the ArtBrew pub at just after 6 pm armed with £30 (£3 a pint) and a sketch pad. They weren't expecting to be busy, so he hadn't put much on. They were saving it all for Saturday. Due to this, the beer selection on the hand pump ran out quite quickly. There were plenty of other choices, so I proceeded to work through his supply of porter. After a short while, the sketch pad came out, and the two victims were happy enough that they bought Shirley and I a couple of beers each. The owner of the place then insisted that the guitar and mandolin came out of their hiding place, so we were set for the evening. All this basically meant that I brewed up my first hangover of the trip but had an excellent evening. This is a pub I will continue coming back to. It's only open Friday evening and Saturday, but it's a good place.

Day 9. Ross-on-Wye. A nice quiet little town down the road from Gloucester. Surprisingly quiet, it was a sweltering Saturday afternoon, too hot to do too much walking, so we just had to repair to a pub. Just off the town centre, across the road from a huge Morrison's, is a gem of a micropub called the Tap House, run by Nigel and his wife, Chris. A good range of beer from dark to light, weak to strong. All are in top condition—some kegs on, cider, gin. Basically most bases are covered. We seemed to be able to strike up conversations with everyone who came there. There's a bunch of middle age+ blokes on a 35-mile hike, a load of women who appeared to be on a hen-do pub crawl but for the fact that there were two men in the group.

The deputy mayor came in for a few beers. I was only aware that he was the deputy Mayor, as I was told after he left. He wasn't up his own behind, being all political. He was just in for a few pints. I'm told he actually physically does stuff for his community rather than talk crap about what he thinks other people should be doing, like some mayors of major cities that I could mention. Another pub that I would go out of my way to come to when we are in the area. He's been going nine months, and it's all going in the right direction. He also seemed interested in having a jam session next time I was around. I'll look forward to that. Keep up the good work.

Day 10. I don't know what it is about Llandrindod Wells –
Church of the holy trinity for those who are interested –
that I always get so wrong. We first came across this
pleasant little town in mid-Wales a couple of years back
and found this excellent micropub, Arvon Ales. It had won
CAMRA pub of Wales in 2016 and served a good range of
dark and light, strong and weak ales, forty different
whiskies and 30 gins. It also has folk music on the 2nd and
4th Sundays and an acoustic jam on the third Sunday. It is
closed on Mondays and Tuesdays. So the second time we
visit the town, it is a Monday (this is when we first realise
it's closed on the first two days of the week), so no Arvon
ales at that visit. This time we thought we'd box clever -
not being aware of the music situation, we decided we
would aim at Sunday. Yippee! It was open. Of course, as
there are normally 4 Sundays in the month, we have a 75%
chance of getting it right. This was the 5th Sunday of the
month. A bit of a no-mans-land in terms of music, so I got
it wrong again. Still a pleasant interlude in a nice town in a
really good pub. The sketchbook came out, and people
were sufficiently impressed that we had beers bought for
us. As an aside, I note that this phone tried to spell check
whisky by adding an 'e'. I didn't think inanimate objects
could be Philistines.

Day 11. Penultimate day and Ludlow in Shropshire.
Something of a disappointment. Not because of Ludlow,

138

just bad timing. Nothing wrong with Ludlow. It has a proper ironmonger, proper butchers and proper clothes shops that will charge you £65 for a £3 t-shirt because it's Ludlow. If you want to see some fantastic-looking old-world pubs, go no further than Ludlow. Inside some of them is like stepping back in time. If you are looking for good beer, go somewhere else. Come on, Ludlow pubs, show some imagination. There is a choice between middle-of-the-road pale ales or middle-of-the-road bitter. It's as dull as ditch water. There's no excuse, they have a good brewery in town, and Salopian brewery isn't that far away. There are some exceptions, but there are severe limitations. Ludlow Brewing co is a good brewery with a pub on site. They have an excellent range of all styles of beer, all in immaculate condition. It closes at 5 pm every day except Friday and Saturday when they stay open 'til 6. There are two micro pubs in town. One is open all week except Monday. The other is open Thursday through Saturday. Therein lies my issue. I landed here on beer desert Monday. A few lunchtime pints at the brewery, then a meal at the Church pub, which really pushes their boat out by putting on an IPA alongside all the other middle-of-the-road stuff. Early night for us, then onto Cambridgeshire in the morning.

Day 12, 17 pubs, 15 towns, 12 days, 11 counties. 1 principality, 1 country, one hangover (not trying hard enough). Our final destination was Little Gransden. Small family-run pub through two generations so far. It has its own brewery called Son of Sid, which brews a perfectly serviceable, if not overly exciting bitter, light pale and a golden ale. It also brews a magnificent Muck Cart Mild. I am not a fan of dark mild, but this one is exceptional. Champion beer of Britain 2012 in its class. It does not sell its beers to anyone other than local fares and other events, so you have to go to Little Gransden if you want any. The pub comprises three small rooms; one with a TV, one for dining (Fridays only) and one for drinking and chatting for those who don't want to watch 22 airheads kicking a windbag around and thinking they are heroes for doing it. (this night was the women's version – almost as tedious as the men's) Being a Tuesday, it was quiet but interesting conversations from all who entered. The landlord was good enough to allow us to park up for the night in his car park, so we were able to settle down and savour their delightful 3.5% flavoursome mild. Homeward bound this morning after a thoroughly enjoyable 12-day pub crawl.

That's your lot. My wife and I continue to cruise around the British Isles looking for interesting pubs. It is an everchanging scene. The larger pubs continue to be mismanaged by profit-chasing landlords who have no interest in the industry. Micropubs are constantly opening and closing. It seems that the people who are opening these small premises for the right reasons are the ones that seem to survive best. The ones that have owners who understand that it is the customers that make the pub, not necessarily the fixtures and fittings. Even themed pubs that have concentrated on the décor to reflect the theme eventually realise that if the pub doesn't work, all the decoration in the world wouldn't make a difference.

If you like a beer and a conversation, seek out these pubs. They are not to everyone's tastes but I always find the good in them. You are never going to lose much in the long run. If you don't like what you see, go somewhere else. All you will have lost is half an hour of your time and the price of a beer. If you do like it, then it can open up a whole world of experiences.

Now read on while I take you into my world of pub conversations.

PART 2

The Bar Room Barrister

Intro

I like a beer. I like going into pubs even more. The British pub is an institution unlike anywhere else in the world. It is not understood by most people who are not from here and a huge section of those who are. Youngsters go to pubs to get drunk and/or find a sexual partner. Older people have a more complicated relationship with these establishments. It is as much, and in my case more, about meeting people and having a conversation. I sometimes go to play music or listen to friends playing music. Sometimes I just want a quiet pint with my wife. In all of this, there are hundreds of hours of interlocution delving into just about everything. Some pubs prefer people not to talk politics or religion because people get a little hot under the collar about these subjects. Add the demon alcohol, and it can get fiery. I have never had a problem, so I ignore the rule.

What follows is a series of short tongue-in-cheek monologues that have come off the back of these conversations. They are not a transcript of one conversation but more an overview of the many all mixed into one. They describe 'what-if scenarios' surrounding actual events that have happened in recent years. This is interspersed with rants about things I find increasingly frustrating in the modern world in which we live. I have no political experience or direct knowledge of the workings of organisations such as Parliament, the media, et al. I am a fabulous barroom barrister and have sorted out the world's troubles many times over while sitting at a bar stool. I mistrust those in the higher echelons of the corridors of power. I am not party political, I think they are all at it, and they have one central policy in mind whenever decisions are made, and that is, 'How will it affect me and my career?' I will also, very unusually, recommend going to the half page conclusion on the last page of this tome and read that before continuing.

I have little knowledge of the workings of the world of news media. They are profit-making organisations, so their first concern is to make that profit. That means writing stories that they need to get people to read, listen to and watch. And 'good news' does not sell copy, so the news media can be pretty negative. Generally speaking, a newspaper article will have a headline giving the reader the story in a few short words. There then follows a paragraph – maybe two – of the salient points that make up the story. The rest is essentially the opinion of the writer or editor. I don't give a toss about the opinions of newspaper editors. I just want them to provide me with the facts so that I can form my own opinions. So I don't take long to read a newspaper: Headline, two paragraphs, next story, crossword, done. I am, despite my lack of knowledge of political machinations, a sentient being. I can read, and I do have opinions. So, where I have created a scenario to demonstrate a point, it needs to be understood that these stories are figments of my imagination. It is my way of trying to make sense of some of the decisions that are made on our behalf by the people we elect to make those decisions. Although the background events are real, what happens behind closed doors in the pages that follow, is not – at least, I don't think they are. The reader can make their own minds up.

All the other rants are my way of expressing my opinion. If the reader does not like the idea that people can have opinions that are different to their own, then this is probably not what you should be reading. I do like a debate. I like to talk to people who do not necessarily agree with my opinion. That is the way I learn stuff. My opinions are not set in stone. They can be changed by good, well-thought-out arguments. This modern habit of saying that because I don't agree with a particular person, I am just going to cancel that person from my life and make believe they don't exist is, in my opinion, very damaging. I certainly don't learn anything from talking to people who agree with everything I say, although I do get to fine-tune some of my thoughts. I don't know how many times I have had a discussion with someone who has said something that I disagreed with. My issue is, as I have no debating experience or skills, I know that I disagree, but I find it challenging to elocute my thoughts until I have had time to digest and consider all the implications. This would typically take a day or so. Not ideal in the heat of a debate, and the impact of putting across your argument will have diminished after a day.

Sitting at a computer, considering all those debates and all the points I wanted to make, seems easier to me. The only drawback is that I don't get the counterargument. It is more of a response to something already said to me and what I wished I had said at the time. I therefore have to content myself with the hope that this will generate conversation, make people who would not normally agree with my point of view think a little more on the subject matter and generally share opinion without worrying about being 'cancelled'.

Before I launch into this, I will say something about religion. I do this here as I do not want to dedicate an entire chapter to this most divisive of subjects. As most of what follows is opinion some of which may offend, I think the reader needs to know where I stand from the start so I

145

will lay my cards out now. It is my belief that we all come from the same place. We are all born and grow from the earth and all the minerals that makes up this huge orb. Then when we die, we go back into the earth. Our mortal remains are broken down and distributed to all living things animal and vegetable. As far as the 'spirit' is concerned, these are electrical impulses caused by synapse connections that are made throughout every individual's lives. They are what makes us all individual. If you want to know what happens to that spirit when you die, think about a light switch and ask where the light goes to when you switch it off.

When dealing with humans, we should all be actively looking for what brings us together as a species. Rejoice in the fact that we all want roughly the same things. What we eat and the various cultures that have been developed over the millennia are purely geographical. Island dwellers were by and large pescatarian, people who lived on vast continents tended towards consumption of herbivorous animals and a more omnivorous diet unless the animals were at a premium in which case the population would have tended towards vegetarianism. The colour of our skin is purely geographical. Those whose ancestors hailed from Africa, South Asia, south and central America where the sun is strong. Required natural protection from the sun's powerful uv rays. Those that hailed from colder climates where the sun is weaker and had a lot more atmosphere to go through, would have lighter skin to allow as much of the sunlight as possible in so that the chemical reactions vital to our survival was enabled. Beneath the skin, everything is the more or less the same. Religion and dietary considerations have been built on from a small group of people who lived in an age when they had no scientific knowledge but knew that some things weren't healthy and wanted their people to live. To do this, they passed down rules telling them they had to comply because their god – whichever one it was – said so. This just cut off any argument before it started and kept people healthy. What religion does nowadays – and I am mainly talking about the middle Eastern ones of Judaism, christianity and Islam – is draw lines in the sand over which we should not step if we do not believe in the rhetoric of that side of the line. All other religions may well do the same, I have little knowledge and no interest in them. Religion divides, it does not bring us all together, it sets us apart. "My God's beard is bigger than your God's beard". It says, "I believe in this set of tenets because that is what I have been taught to believe and the only thing I have to back this up with is blind faith." Be religious if you want to be. I have no problem with anyone who wants or needs it to get them through the day, especially if it makes them a better person. But don't tell me that religion is a force for good in the world. There are too many examples

– amongst them, the most serious crimes against humanity – to count that show this to be on the opposite end of the scale to absolute truth or honesty. Remember, no one ever went to war under the flag of atheism. More people have died, been maimed and tortured as a direct result of wars caused by religious rhetoric – whichever hat they choose to wear – than any other cause, so it's not for me.

In conclusion, believe what you want to believe, but allow others the same latitude. If you want me to show respect for your beliefs, show respect for mine. I have to say that this doesn't happen much. I find Christian churches demanding that I show respect when walking into a church but refuse to even acknowledge my belief system – or if they do, they just think that I am wrong. I have never entered a Mosque, but I am always hearing about people being threatened by the zealots within that faith if they show disrespect for their church while again, refusing to acknowledge other belief systems. Look for things that bring all the peoples of the world together instead of separating as is the modern way.

So that has got that out of the way.

Before I get into those conversations, I want to tell a story. This first scenario is something that I wrote in 2012 in response to stuff that was happening in the press at the time. It is interesting to me that nothing has really been resolved 11 years later. It has all just gone back behind closed doors. □

A FOETID STENCH

The story starts circa 2011 and involves politicians, the media and the police in a three-way finger-pointing match. In my mind, the circumstances dovetail far too neatly to be anything other than linked.

Let us make this absolutely clear. This is a fictional account using actual events as a backdrop. It is the product of my own imagination. I have cunningly altered names to throw the reader off the scent if they start thinking that this is about a living individual. We must remember that most fiction writers will use real situations as inspiration or as a backdrop for their storytelling. This is no different to that. Some people may read this and draw parallels to individuals that are involved in current situations. I have no personal knowledge of how political current affairs are handled in the corridors of power, only what I read in the newspapers, and we know how they can distort facts. Any parallels that are drawn are done at the readers' own risk. I cannot take responsibility for other people's wild imaginations.

This is a story that, on the surface, is one of a businessman getting too big for his boots and a politician trying to knock him off his perch. The more one thinks about it, though, the more the foetid stench of political manoeuvrings seems to rise up and infect the entire sorry mess. We will start by introducing the two main protagonists (or is that 'antagonists'). The third party is the higher echelons of the police service and, as such, the whipping boys of the other two.

The first is a person of foreign extraction but of European lineage - shall we call him Paddington (Paddy to his friends if he has any?) He decided that he would quite like to own a newspaper. Being a pushy sort, he got his way and worked his way up the international hierarchy within the media world. Eventually, he got so high that he bashed his head on the metaphorical glass ceiling and found that he could rise no further. Not being one to accept such barriers, he decided to break the glass ceiling. (Glass is good like that. Very brittle, easy to break). Having overcome this barrier, he continued to rise until he was the most influential media mogul in the world and found once again that he could advance no further. Again, these sorts of barriers annoy him. He now spends his time working out how to get more. What does one do when one has all that power? Look for more, obviously! What does one do when you own half of the media? Aim for all of it, obviously. If you aim for the moon and only get halfway, you are neither here nor there. If you aim for the stars and only get halfway, if nothing else, you are way beyond the moon. We should also recognise that this is not about money. If one has more money than they can ever spend, it makes not a jot of difference if you make more. What does matter is power. So, this is all about power.

Now there are a lot of very powerful people out there that politicians either do not worry about or who they actively associate with. Tiny Rowlands of Lonrho in the '70s and '80s and Oppenheimer of Anglo-American were two prime examples. There are many current examples today. Politicians are happy with these people. They employ, they create wealth, they grease palms, and everyone is happy. Okay, they may be a little shady, and some of the ways they do things are not always morally correct, but as long as no one is getting hurt – or at least if they are, we are blissfully ignorant of the suffering caused – then who is going to argue. Or, of course, if it is the wronguns that get it, where's the problem?

The media, on the other hand, is another story. If all the media were of one mind, they could change governments just by bombarding the newspapers and TV with negativity. This area of business has always been one of the most powerful and influential of all. It doesn't matter where in the world you are; control of the media will get ambitious people everything they need. But there must be some way of creating balance. In the media, that is

152

achieved by making sure that they all have differing agenda. If one person were to have a controlling influence and, therefore, one agenda, checks and balances would be lost.

There isn't a politician in the world who would accept this... unless it was to their advantage, of course. So, when our foreign friend started making moves to take over the controlling share of the media, the politicians would have found this unacceptable! The question is, what do they do about it? They can't prevent someone from carrying out legitimate business. They can't nationalise the media – although some politicians would prefer that option. There is a Labour Government in power during this period that is distinctly right-of-centre, dealing with a media mogul that appears to support them. This causes a problem. They have a tough decision, but they cannot allow Paddy to become too powerful. Not in the media.

This brings us neatly to our second player—a politician. In this scenario, we will refer to this person as 'politician' because the individual changes halfway through due to the inconvenience of a general election and a change of political hue.

Let us face it; politicians in the higher echelons of power and those whose ambitions would take them there, are a

153

dishonest lot. The only reason that they can climb the greasy pole is because they are themselves slimy. They connive, they scheme, they make sure others take the fall for their cockups. They get other people to make decisions and adopt them as their own if it turns out to be a good one. Plenty of distance can be created if it goes the other way. The best of them are always deniable. Take on a politician, and you must be dirtier than they, and there are none too many people who can boast that.

Let us now take a look at the issues that make up this story. There are three sides, as I have mentioned, so there are three issues. One is the expenses scandal, where the media picked up on politicians claiming expenses for spurious reasons. On the other hand, there was the media who were found to be illegally tapping people's phones. As far as the police are concerned, during all this, there are allegations that they were accepting bribes from the media for information. Three issues that are seemingly separate but, at the same time, inextricably linked.

We'll have a look at the expenses scandal. Who honestly did not think that politicians from all sides of the political divide were making dodgy expense claims and have been for years? Even I, with my serious lack of political knowledge, was aware of many of them sharing office space in Westminster with their colleagues and therefore

154

sharing the costs. All MPs are entitled to claim for office space, bearing in mind that the majority have constituencies miles outside London. It would be unreasonable to expect working constituency politicians to carry out their legitimate political duties within Westminster without somewhere to work. The problem came when they shared their office space but claimed rent allowance as if they were paying the full whack. This is standard practice, I'm told. Strange that nothing has been said about this. It couldn't possibly be that the whips that are investigating this are doing the same thing. To bring this to light would seriously damage their expenditure. The main thrust of the expenses allegations was greedy public servants getting their household bills and entertainment paid out of the public purse.

Because the media got hold of information relating to the abuse of expenses, they started making noises. Parliament had to be seen to do something about it. This is all well and good, but the bright spark who decided to get the police involved in the 'scandal', caused a furore in the corridors of power and many politicians ended up finding themselves contemplating their navels in Ford Open Prison or having a very uncomfortable time waiting for justice to take its course. This caused a lot of friction between the police and politicians. When they got the police involved, it was thought that the investigating officers would just go

155

through the motions but ultimately do as they were told, find nothing untoward and then go away. In the event, to the horror of many, they actually investigated the problem correctly. This was not in the script for most parliamentarians, as it meant that the police kept on dragging up uncomfortable facts about what had been common practice for centuries. This was how politicians had always augmented their perfectly reasonable salaries since the dawn of time. Let us consider that in 2022, we have had eleven years since they have lost this little 'perk'. In all those intervening years, they have been giving themselves 11% per annum pay increases. Way above the inflation rate and four or five times above any other publicly funded organisation. This couldn't possibly be politicians taking up the slack of their lost income by just taking out of the public purse in full view, could it?

There has also been a lot of rubbish about things like subsidised canteen food. I believe this is just a non-profit making arrangement. So yes, they do get subsidised grub, but not at the expense of Joe public. The real issue is the amount they can claim for food outside the parliament building. As a public-funded organisation, they don't have to spend hundreds on a single meal in the guise of 'entertainment'. This should be capped. Of course, the Media have been, by and large, of one mind on this issue. Politicians spending public money on personal items need to be scrutinised, and if they are being unreasonable, their claims should be refused. Politicians had been unable to extricate themselves from the media scrutiny during this period. Imagine if the purveyors of our news were of one mind in all subjects. The upshot is that, once the police got involved, they put politicians' noses out, and politicians hold the purse strings of the police. Politicians are always going to have the last word.

Okay, so we know who the players are, and we know what the issues are. How do they dovetail, and what is making me scratch my head over this? This is the really fictional part. This is where I have considered facts and come to my own fanciful conclusions.

Now, this politician is faced with a media mogul who is getting to the point where he could theoretically control political changes through his media outlets. So what does the establishment do about this? How do they deal with this anomaly? Well, how about this for a scenario that will please the conspiracy theorist in all of us and also allow us to wag our righteous fingers at the nasty politicians, nasty media and nasty police..

The Scenario

Over the course of the previous year or so, it had been becoming increasingly evident that some media outlets had information that no one else had. Some of it was personal and would only have been known personally to an individual and their immediate circle. So how were the media getting their information? It couldn't have been legal. They seemed to have been in places where they would have heard this information first-hand. There is only one reasonable conclusion. Subterfuge! Phone tapping, surveillance, getting to listen to conversations without the victim being aware. The age of rummaging through dustbins has all but been consigned to the history books. There are so many other ways of getting the information needed.

Our politician – and we are talking high up in the pecking order – has considered the issue of our media mogul and his steady rise to power. The problem is that a balance needs to be maintained in the media so that the public gets a range of different commentaries. This politician, in his capacity as a public servant, sidles up to our media mogul, Paddy, and tells him that the government are not too happy about his manoeuvrings. The advice offered to him is that it would be in his and everyone else's best interests to back out at this early stage. Stop with his ambitions to take over the media world and control the power strings. There are no overt threats, no histrionics, just advice to 'back off and keep what you have now.'

Paddy, who is not used to taking 'advice', thinks to himself, 'Who does he think he is, trying to cut me off before I have got started?!' He cannot conceive of any scenario that involves taking this advice. In fact, the temerity of this jumped-up political nobody incenses him to the point where he believes that upping the ante is the only way forward. 'Since when do politicians think they can run the country without my consent?' A plan will have to be put into place to make a power grab within the media world and bring this fool down a peg or two.

Our politician is not surprised by this. This reaction would have been anticipated, and measures put on standby to deal with it. It would have to be something that will hurt our friend Paddy without getting the rest of the media adversely involved. Of course, the rest of the media aren't particularly enamoured with Paddy because they are in danger of being side-lined if he gets too powerful. Nor are they without blame. This can only mean that they are potential allies for the politicians. One's enemy's enemy is one's friend. Politicians are always trying to get the media on side, so they are well-practised at it, if not consistently all that successful. The media would need to be aware of what the politicians want to do so that they can ensure

159

that they don't get caught in the same net. At the same time, it needs to be made known that it is in the interests of the media, in general, to stay on message. That going outside of the political brief could inhibit the strategy. So they really do need to be on side and in agreement.

It only remains to put into place the plan. In this case, it surrounds the phone hacking issue that has already been rumbling on in the background. Nice and simple. It is illegal, so Paddy can't tell people that he wasn't dishonest. He is in ultimate control of his empire, so the old 'I was not told' or 'I didn't know' wouldn't work. And it was happening, so getting proof would be easy enough. The only thing they had to do, was to make sure the rest of the media could duck out of the way. They are involved up to their grubby necks themselves, but they aren't becoming dangerous. They are, however, allies and a potentially useful tool in this scheme.

So a little snippet gets out to the press that Paddy's newspaper journalists are hacking phones. Nothing too over-the-top. Just a few politicians and celebs sticking parts of their anatomy where they don't belong. Slowly dial it up. Suggest that the private personal information could only have come from foul means rather than fair. Perhaps get one or two celebrities and politicians to make a fuss on TV. Stir up a mini media frenzy so that everyone can beat their breasts about it. Get it to a point where there is a definite offence being alleged.

This is where our third party gets involved. The politician has to ensure that the police are involved, preferably at a high level. The Anti-terrorist Branch would do. They use phone hacking in their business, and they can just about get away with justifying an investigation. But the politician has an end game, and the police are pawns in this little power play. Someone is going to get burnt, and it isn't going to be any politician. In fact, the police are probably going to walk into this trap with their eyes wide open, knowing what it is but being powerless to do anything about it.

Ensuring the story is getting plenty of media attention has the effect of making sure that there is a senior police officer involved. Nothing like a bit of screen time to get senior police officers out of bed. This should be easy enough. Any Deputy Assistant Commissioner (DAC) or above are looking at the top job. Most will do as they are told if that carrot was dangled in front of their noses. The great thing about all ambitious people is that one will always get productivity out of them while having leverage. Especially if you are the one who holds the key to their ambitions.

The politician ensures that an investigation is started and will then allow it to progress to a point and then pull the plug. It cannot look like the plug has been pulled by a politician. It has to be a decision taken by the police without a whiff of political interference. Essentially, the police will be told that there is too much going on, what with the 7/7 and the 21/7 London bombings and the current critical terrorist threat level. Investigating a few dodgy phone hacks about celebrity infidelity is not good use of police resources. So the DAC is cornered into making a decision that he would prefer not to make. He has his ambitions to think about, so it will not take long to come to the right one. The investigation is therefore pulled at the behest of the DAC due to 'ongoing heightened threat levels.' It is crucial from the politician's point of view that this is the decision of the police to end the investigation. Remain deniable is the mantra, just in case. Throwing the odd police officer to the wolves when things go tits-up is never a bad thing and is often good for political kudos. Once this has been done, our politician is in a position where they can sidle up to Paddy once again and tell him that it would really be in his best interest to back off. This was a little demonstration of what could be if he was not going to be reasonable.

The politician believes they are in a position of strength now. He has half an investigation that was conducted by police. He has a police decision to stop the investigation, and he knows he has something on his adversary.

Paddy is watching all of this unfold. He is aware that the police have been investigating his practises. He is also aware that he could never be able to justify it to an enquiry if it got that far. He thinks about this for a while. This sort of thing is not what he expects of politicians. They should be dancing to his tune. He needs a more significant share of the media. He has a little pow-wow with his top people. He is not trying to mitigate any potential fallout. He is more aggressive than that! He will be planning his next move.

In the meantime, there is a change of government, one that has a weakened mandate. From Paddy's point of view, this is excellent news. A new broom with virtually no bristles is just the sort of politician that he loves. This should make it easier for him to throw his weight around. He is thinking that the politicians have picked on the wrong bloke. He is not used to being told! He decides to call their bluff. The bluff, after all, was issued by the previous incumbent, and the new one will not have been adequately briefed. Where is the risk? Would the politicians really do this thing and try to weaken his position? If they did, in Paddy's mind, they would have to bring the entire media industry to its knees. Let's face it, if

Paddy is doing it, then so is everyone else. If he gets pulled down, the whole house of cards will have to tumble. And who else would follow? How many politicians would come crashing down? No! It's a bluff. And how do you answer a bluff? There is only one way. Go for the jugular! Be aggressive! Make a decisive move! So he decides to make a move on getting control of 60% of the TV news coverage. Along with his newspaper empire, this would make him unstoppable!

Paddy is bull-headed. He has become successful by confronting issues head-on. He is too arrogant to believe that anyone would slip under his radar. Nor does he ever consider that no one will have his back watched. He is the hunter. He is looking at what is in front of him. Bread and butter to your top politician. If Paddy is the hunter, the politician is the aggressive scavenger ready to attack the hunter and take them off the kill.

Now, our brand new, fresh-out-the-box politician sees this happening and is genuinely narked off that it has come to this. He is of a different political hue to the one who started the ball rolling, but when it comes to media power, there is no compromise and very little difference in how they deal with transgressors. Everything has been set up nicely. Paddy wants to play hardball, so let's shake this particular sports bag and see what falls out. This has to be thought out carefully. The new politician will be of the same opinion as the outgoing one with regard to the importance of limiting the amount of power being wielded by one person in the media. There is no doubt that Paddy is not going to capitulate easily, and he is a wily character, so this has to be thought out.

What the politician does not want is a huge splash of revelations all at once. That would not do the trick. A big strong storm that will blow out in a couple of days is not what we have in mind here - oh no! Paddy could ride that storm without a backward glance and come out the other end stronger. He reverts to the original strategy with a view to taking it further this time. A little story about phone hacking here, another revelation there, build momentum and make each one a little worse. Build to a crescendo. Ensure that the public is going to be horrified. Make sure that the victims of the phone hacking (because we are still running with this) are going to pull at the public heartstrings. We can have a few celebrities involved, but better to have vulnerable children or an innocent good Samaritan being subject to the nasty media attention. Make sure the rest of the media are behind us. What better than to have the media pumping out revelations about the nastiness of the media? Newspapers hacking victims of murder and terrorist atrocities? That will do nicely! Young, innocent murder victims that have been subject to media attention in the recent past? That would be even better.

Once all this is starting to gain momentum, our politician can then stick his head above the pulpit and say, 'Let's have a public enquiry.' Let us face it, when the word 'public' is mentioned in this context, we are talking media circus with bells on. He then asks prominent members of Paddy's staff to explain how they got their information. Of course, Paddy will have a strategy. One that would involve taking someone else down with him and, if he plays it right, getting them to take the entire wrap. Bringing into question the integrity of the police is always a good wheeze. Bribery and corruption in the least corrupt police force on earth (according to the police anyway). Now things are coming out that suddenly adds power to the political establishment's elbow. No one would have expected anyone to admit to bribing police for information. How outrageous! How well played - right into the hands of our scheming politician! This means that he has more offences. He also has the other set of fall guys – the police.

Oh, and he will have to get the police involved again. This is fantastic. All of his colleagues across the political spectrum are still smarting about the expenses investigation, so they are more than happy for a little payback. How is he going to manage that after the investigation into the phone hacking has already revealed that there was nothing of importance to investigate? The public doesn't know that it was a political decision to stop the investigation, so it can remain a police decision. All they now have to do is cast aspersions about the making of that decision. Come across as being outraged that the investigation was stopped without getting to the bottom of it. Make sure that everyone knows that this is an example of police incompetence. Perhaps get a presiding judge to have his two pen'uth and point towards police incompetence. They don't need evidence; everyone is always ready to believe that the police couldn't investigate their way out of a room with one door with a big 'exit' sign on it. They can take the fall for it. He can be self-righteous and ask searching questions about why they did such a botched job of the first investigation. Throw in the idea that bribery was involved without being too specific, bearing in mind that bribery was not, in fact, a factor in that decision but it would tie in quite nicely to the revelations made by Paddy's crew. This would force their hand into reopening the investigation. In addition, as the previous investigation was dropped so publicly, the opening of this one can be equally as public. All the while, everyone is asking why the police were taking bribes from the media! In particular, Paddy's media! Their credibility is shot. They are in a hole, and they have forgotten to stop digging. The rest of the media are doing a fine job in both dragging up more revelations on Paddy and trashing the police. They have to do this because, if they are not seen to be damning of these dodgy media practices, will they be next in the firing line? As far as attacking police, well, that is their bread and butter. Nothing sells copy better than to catch the police out breaking the rules they are supposed to be enforcing. Anyway, as far as the politicians are concerned, it serves them right for investigating their perfectly reasonable expense claims.

So the enquiry goes ahead. Prominent members of Paddy's staff are paraded across our television screens and newspapers. Some lost their jobs, although I doubt they would be destitute after their golden handshake and their enhanced employability in the wake of media exposure. Although they would probably be able to live out their lives in comfort without employment. A long-established newspaper that dealt with titillation and gossip has gone. Closed down by the boss as having no place in today's society.

A couple of police officers have bitten the metaphorical bullet. In political terms, they are ten a penny, especially the commissioned ranks. Anyone of DAC or above will be looking for the top position and will bend over and take whatever they are told to take if they want that top position.

Then there is the rest of the media. So far, they have managed to slip away from the limelight. That old mantra 'never become part of the story' ringing loudly in their ears. We all know that they were as bad as anyone else, but we need a healthy media who take different sides. They then effectively cancel themselves out, allowing politicians to get on with their shenanigans.

The three elements of this story are being treated by the general public as shocking. As if most people didn't know that the media resorted to less-than-honest ways of getting to a story. Anyone who was horrified by the 'revelations' of the expenses scandal are either kidding themselves or have been living on another planet. And people bribing police? I never witnessed it personally, but I wouldn't be surprised if low-level bribery by the media were happening among the higher ranks and civilian staff – I can't see PC Plod having enough information of any value to get a media person excited. If they get caught, that's fine by me. They wouldn't get any kind of a golden handshake. Maybe they could be looking at a little free bed and breakfast at his majesty's pleasure. You make your bed; you sleep in it.

As for Paddy and his corporation, he went quiet for a while. The bid to take over the TV side of the media is on hold if not dead in the water. He wouldn't have liked dropping it, but it was the only expedient thing to do. He may even have more tricks up his sleeve. The newspaper that crashed and burned as a result of all of this had a following, and now there was a gap in the market that has since been filled by social media and easy access to porn sites – making newspapers like that something of a relic from a bygone age. We wait with breath abated to see what the next move will be. It is Paddy's turn to make a move. Did he knock his king over and concede? Unlikely. He is still moving and shaking and trying to guide political opinion to his will. He may perhaps sacrifice a few more pawns in order to manoeuvre himself back into a position of strength. (He wouldn't want to sacrifice any more major players, no one would want to work for him if that happened). I have no doubt that it will be something, and I think it will creep up on us, and I would say that the other media companies better be on their mettle. He has no allegiances. He has been taken apart, and his media rivals have been complicit. He will want them to have their comeuppance. He was, after all, not doing anything that they weren't doing, so why should they walk away with a smug look on their face?

Watch this space

EUROPE

Ah, Europe. What can we say about this subject that has not been said ad nauseum? The European Commission, the European Parliament, the euro, wine lakes, food mountains and, of course, Brexit. It is a never-ending mess created for, by and on behalf of politicians. Ya gotta luv 'em.

I will start this by saying that I like Europe and Europeans. Even the French! And even the French don't like the French. I wouldn't say that they were all perfect, but then that would be ridiculous. The human species has a full mix of good, bad and indifferent across the board. Borders, religion and skin tone, do not affect that. We in this country do, after all, come from the same mix as our European brethren. Celts and Picts started us off, iechyd da'ing everyone to within an inch of their lives. Then the Romans, circa 2000 years ago, decided that we didn't speak enough Latin, so they sauntered over to correct that, starting off with 'Veni vidi vici', apparently. The Romans got bored and slinked off to be replaced by the Angles and the Saxons who thought they might try to tame this wild island and change our language to English. Then the Vikings felt the need to teach Yorkshire people how to say 'Hey oop lad' and 'Eee ba gum' so they came with their la-de-da personal hygiene and charmed all the women

172

away from the Celt/German/Roman unhygienic men who only bathed once a year whether they needed to or not. Then it was the turn of the French. In fact, they were also Norsemen who had invaded France and had become French. I'm not sure how accurate my memory is, but apparently, in 1066, a bloke called Harry, who had red hair and a matching beard and constantly moaned about media intrusion, went to a place called Battle, where he picked a fight with a bloke called Norman who had come from France. Norman had decided that we all needed to speak French, so he had landed in Pevensey near Hastings and went looking for Battle as the best place to start teaching the language. Norman then shot Harry in the eye with an arrow then went off to build a load of castles which he called Norman after himself. This was all quite thirsty work, so he went to a pub called William the Conqueror, where he had a glass of wine – he was French, the French didn't know anything about good beer. He liked the pub so much that he named himself after the pub and went to live in Canterbury. There he made French the language of the court. And they all didn't live happily ever after.

Loads of Europeans – mainly French, Dutch and Spanish – have attempted and failed since. The fact is that all these invaders became part of us, lived with us, bred with us and became us. So we are as European as bratwurst in a paella with pasta on the side, and baklava for pud, cooked by a Cordon Bleu chef. We now have a global movement of people, so we have the wonderful advantage of Asian and African influences to add sparkle to our DNA, but that's another story.

If we look at Europe over the last few centuries, it seems that several attempts have been made to unite it as one single entity. Napoleon thought that it would be easier if the whole of Europe was run by one person – him. That way, apparently, wars wouldn't start. So, how does he think he is going to achieve this nirvana? By going to war. Didn't work. Bismarck had a few squabbles, but that did not appear to be about unifying Europe. He did, however, unify Germany, bringing together Prussia, Bavaria and many minor Germanic states – including, controversially, Schleswig/Holstein, which is still to this day disputed by some Danes – under his umbrella. Interestingly, he deliberately excluded Austria.

Kaiser Wilhelm then wanted a bigger Germany, and so tried to take over France in the4 second decade of the twentieth century. Who knows where he would have gone from there if he had succeeded? Fortunately, he didn't, but not before he had sacrificed millions of ordinary men, women and children. Then a certain psychopathic lunatic tried to forcibly unite Europe in the 1930s and 40s.

Ambitions to unite Europe never diminished despite so many abject failures. Still, in the mid-to-late 20th century, politicians took the view that a more peaceful, inclusive way was needed to unite the continent. They never for a moment thought that all these failures probably indicated that we were happier squabbling than being in a brotherly – or sisterly – embrace. The European Common Market, the European Economic Community (EEC), The European Union (EU) and all the political manoeuvrings is the result of that.

As far as the Common Market is concerned, I have to admit to a certain amount of an ambivalent attitude. As previously mentioned, I have no love of politicians. I do believe that we are all Europeans. This is geography, we have no choice in the matter, but I question why politicians have to get involved. Europe is something of a community already. We have squabbled with one another, invaded and counter-invaded each other countless times. We have supported some who have been invaded but ignored others. We have travelled, visited, holidayed in all the countries of Europe and taken positives and negatives away when we left. None of this has changed. The only reason we have gone to war with each other is because politicians and religious zealots couldn't talk through their problems, and so they thought it appropriate to sacrifice ordinary people to drive home their own personal points of view. Take politicians and religion out of the system, and we won't see a cessation of all violence, that wouldn't be in our nature as humans, but I would say that it would be much smaller in scale and localised.

What we appeared to have had ended up with, is what the supporters believed to be an all-singing, all-dancing system that benefits all and what detractors believed to be a millstone around our necks. I get the feeling that we were somewhere in the middle, and we, as Europeans, can't decide how to identify ourselves. We are not one country under one government like the USA. We are a bunch of fiercely independent countries with differing ways of seeing things. We want to govern ourselves as individual countries but also be a part of a larger community like a protective coat around us. This seems to be an admirable desire. Unfortunately, we got politicians involved, and it is now just a political toy for our esteemed 'leaders' to play with. It's falling apart at the seams. Not that it can't be fixed. I just feel that getting rid of these pointless Eurocrats would be a good start.

The system started with a handful of countries – Germany, France, Italy, Belgium, Netherlands and Luxemburg – aligning themselves with each other under the banner of a united Europe. Other countries like the UK tagged on later. They had a European parliament and a commission set up to manage common finances and mediate any disputes. The people who made up the commission were unelected officials with political backgrounds. They were a small group and answerable to no one. Rumblings in the UK started up about these unelected bureaucrats and gained momentum during Blair's premiership. There was a perception that the Commission was becoming too dictatorial. They appeared to many to be making decisions that elected officials should be making, and they were getting a little too powerful. What about the European Parliament? They have been around since the 1950s. What are they there for and why aren't they making some of these decisions?

The European Parliament is, to my mind, a politicians' club where they can all get together with their ridiculously generous European allowances and live the high life while doing very little to earn it. MEPs, when they existed in this country, were conspicuous by their absence. They certainly didn't represent anyone that I know of. It's a very expensive club, and it is paid for by the ordinary folk of the European member states. There were even MEPs that were on the leavers' side of the debate when brexit finally came. It comes to something when a person who is on the inside and therefore knows what goes on in there feels that the system is so bad that they campaign themselves out of their own job.

The question I have always asked is, what is the role of the European Parliament? The commission was clearly ignoring the parliament and going in its own direction. Surely the parliament – an elected body – would be better placed. Here is the issue. A parliament exists, among other things, to create and maintain legislation, collect and distribute wealth through taxation, ensure health and sanitation is maintained and protect their borders. Each country within the EU has its own parliament to do just this. Of course, while there may not be any physical borders under normal circumstances, they can be re-invoked at a moment's notice as demonstrated by the recent covid pandemic. So what does the European Parliament do? It says it's there to create and maintain legislation, but why? We already have those systems in place in each individual member state. The commission is there to ensure that all the members have roughly similar laws. I know some legalities may need to be clarified if we are dealing with many different countries with effectively no borders. Having a body of experts to deal with issues involving the differing legislation that each country has is fine, but a full-time parliament? One person suggested to me that they were responsible for the Human Rights system that we have in place. But is it? HR became a real

178

issue during the second world war and mutterings about some sort of a charter to protect human rights started. Europe decided to do something about it. They decided to have a European Convention on Human Rights (ECHR) involving the 47 members of the Council of Europe, They went to each member state to see what each had in place. They put together a document in 1949 to which all member states were to adhere.

Most member states already had similar systems in place. Some were slightly stronger, some much weaker. The commission had put all these systems together, and those people that were there to create legislation on behalf of the Union, came up with something roughly in the middle. What they came up with wasn't even enforceable. Just guidance, apparently. Each individual country had to then go away and come up with their own laws to reflect the commission's findings. During the nineties and early twenty first century, with the proliferation of personal computers, social media and access to all information worldwide, HR became every much to the forefront of European policy. The UK, which did not have a specific act in place but had legislation dealing with all the relevant areas built into each enactment, had systems in place that exceeded the requirements of the commission. In 1998, an act of parliament dealing with HR was enacted which put everything we already had into a single enforceable framework. Much of it was a straight lift from the ECHR document. However, the rights we had in place prior to 1998 have diminished to come into line with Europe. Our right to silence when questioned by police, for example, is reduced (admittedly to a better system). What police can arrest people for has changed. These changes aren't huge, but they are there, and they were more robust before the commission published its eight-part report. Even the report has since been watered down. I believe it was part six that dealt with law and punishment and stated that no person could be punished except by a properly appointed, independent judge at a properly appointed tribunal or trial. The last time I looked, that had been watered down and as a result, if I park my car in a car park, a completely privately owned company working on behalf of the landowner – and therefore not independent – has the ability to issue fines that are almost impossible to fight. If it is contested, it is referred to a 'panel'. Who they are is anyone's guess, but they are unlikely to be independent. They then claim that it should be dealt with as a civil debt if the issue is still contested. It just isn't. It is a fine. A punishment issued by a private company. If it was a civil debt, then they would be demanding the price of the parking charge and not a hugely inflated fine. I think this suggestion that the European Commission were responsible for the UK having policies on HR does not hold water. Rather than strengthening anything we may have had, it has diminished it.

My over-arching question, I suppose, is why do we need politicians to oversee a united Europe of distinctly separate countries? We either have separate countries that cooperate with each other and have whatever restrictions – or lack thereof – that they feel appropriate, or we have a fully-fledged united Europe under one parliament. I can't see that being an option at the moment. There is too strong a national identity in most of the countries, but it could be a future consideration. I see no reason for the very expensive white elephant that is the European Parliament.

Brexit

Now we move onto to Brexit. I feel that I need to reiterate the fact that, although, in the following passages, the background did happen, the closed-door meetings and decisions that follow are fictional. Just me trying to make sense of the nonsense.

Towards the end of Blair's reign (and I use that word advisedly), mutterings started being aired about the European Union and the general discontent that some in the country had. Blair wasn't interested. He wasn't going to let go of the union. That was one of his options for when he stepped down from UK politics. In fact, I would not be surprised if he wanted it even more centralised, with him eventually being the top Euro-johnny-banana. Rather than reassuring the public and countering their complaints with good, solid, well-argued reasons for staying in, he just said, 'I'm the boss, do as you are told.' And shut down the argument. Of course, this just meant more mutterings that got louder and louder. Blair was seeing his personal ratings bombing and saw the writing on the wall. There was Labour in-fighting. No one could agree on anything. The Chancellor was panicking and emptying out the coffers to try and get people back on side. Blair, being a consummate politician (not a compliment) and, sensing real danger, turned to Brown and said, 'Here's the keys, I'm off, Bye.' And left the sinking ship to whoever was chosen to lose the next election.

In the meantime, the people who run the Tory party behind the scenes have been grooming Cameron for years. They see an opportunity. At the next election, the Tories will win. It's a shoo-in. The labour party have all but given up hope. So they place him at the head of an aimless Tory party. Cameron, in the days before he had his spine metaphorically surgically removed, could smell blood with

182

this dysfunctional Labour Party and an increasingly vociferous public questioning the validity of European membership. It was easy. Promise to deal with the European issue if he gained power. What he was saying is that he would listen to the public where the Labour Party was refusing to.

The BBC took to their tried and tested method. Stop and interview what they say are random people in the street. Sometimes they may even have chosen their interviewees. They then conduct what appears to be an impromptu interview with them about whatever it is they want to get opinion on. The person sending the message that the BBC want to deliver is invariably a highly educated, eloquent person with a well-formed argument. The other point of view is represented by a person who can barely tie their own shoelaces, is uneducated and has no clearly formed viewpoint. This is the BBC's idea of balance. I saw this in action back in the 80s when they were doing reports on the apartheid regime in South Africa. One would think this is not a complex argument to get across, and any debate would easily be won. But no, BBC needed to over-egg the pudding by interviewing a person who had a doctorate and was an expert in African History, so could speak with authority on the anti-apartheid subject. The other interviewee was a farmhand in the middle of the Transvaal who had been brought up on a diet of backwards-thinking

183

Dutch Reform Christianity that had them believing that black people were a lower lifeform. He was uneducated and unable to put a coherent sentence together. There was no contest, but it was unnecessary, and it left me wondering why they would want to do it like that. What are they hiding? If you have an obvious argument but want balance, then have balance. Interview proper people who have coherent arguments. Then argue them. To get back to the point, the BBC started canvassing opinion from the Great British public, but only in a way that supported their standpoint trying to steer the public away from coming out of the union.

A general election was held. Despite the Labour Party being in disarray, the Tories only scraped past the post without an overall majority. For Cameron to have such a narrow victory in that political climate must have been a concern for his puppeteers, but he was in, and the European question wasn't going away. In fact, it was getting louder. I find it curious that no politician, even at this point, approached the lectern to try to give the public positive reasons for their position in the union. He just seemed to let it fester. He offered negative reasons for what he thought may happen if we left, but nothing positive to reassure the public that staying in was good for everyone. His reasons started to become clear as they approached the next General Election. An alliance with the

LibDems had been negotiated because of their lack of a clear majority. The coalition probably helped to prevent many of the more damaging right-wing policies from getting past the first post, but it almost destroyed the LibDem Party. In any case, the Tories had to shake the LibDem millstone around their neck, so they would campaign on Europe by telling everyone he would allow the people to decide. The LibDems were fervent Europhiles so Cameron used this. He promised that he would try to sort the problems out and if he couldn't, then he would offer a referendum so that the people of the country could decide for themselves. Many people think having a referendum was the wrong decision. They question the validity of referenda and believe that elected representatives are there to make the hard calls. On the basic facts, I don't think he had a choice. There was a big groundswell of people who were discontented. If we truly have a democracy of the people, for the people etc, and there are that many people who are discontented, it's hard to properly argue and it is a good way to gauge the temperature. It is pointless to say you are in charge; make a decision. If half the people in the entire country are going to disagree with your decision whichever way it goes, then put it to them; that's democracy. It doesn't have to be only once every five years.

So this pompous, thoroughly dislikeable and latterly spineless individual is elected to the premiership in his own right and without the LibDems nipping at his ankles. He immediately sets about honouring his promise and starts the debate ahead of the vote. I don't know what was going through the minds of those who wanted to remain in the EU. Maybe they subscribed to this view that it was a shoo-in for the remain vote to win. Perhaps they were secretly leavers and sabotaged the whole thing. It is certainly inconceivable that the position espoused by Boris Johnson and Nigel Farage, two people who I wouldn't trust to run a bath, much less a country, would somehow convince so many people.

Cameron started by trying to convince the European parliament that there were issues that needed to be sorted out and that the UK would want to vote on this subject if their concerns were not at least considered. The answer was 'Non!' They would not even talk about it. This was the system. Take it or leave it. Now I do have a problem with this. I believe that if they had at least taken the time to consider the issues, it may have been a different story. Whether this was just Cameron's inept negotiating skills or the intransigence of the Europeans, I don't know. I suspect a little of both. No one can tell me any system is perfect, and a little fine-tuning is always beneficial, so not even entertaining the possibility that there was a problem was wrong.

If they had dealt with it properly when the mutterings started, perhaps that situation would never have arisen. Given that it started two PMs down the line, he was only partially to blame for that. In any event, Cameron returned with his tail between his legs. Apparently, the Europeans felt that their system was perfect as it was. Not their finest hour, I would say. They should take some of the responsibility for the whole Brexit debacle. What this means is that it has now become apparent that attempts to deal with the concerns of the dissenting UK public have fallen on deaf ears before it has even started. So, referendum it is. The 'remain' campaign sit around the table to strategize:

PM   How are we going to fight this campaign?

Adviser   I don't see why we should bother. If people can't see it for themselves that staying in European is beneficial to all, what hope do we have? What do you have in mind?

PM   Ease of travel in Europe?

Adviser   Yeah, we could go on about that. But it is obvious, and the leavers will counter with the fact that the Europeans are still going to want UK residents to spend money in Europe. Why would they make it difficult? And it's only one border control for access to all of Europe, so it isn't going to be that much of a problem. We do it whenever we go to every country outside Europe and don't complain or find issue with it. So we will strengthen their campaign by playing into their hands.

PM   What about free trade?

Adviser   Same again, and the leavers will counter with the idea that they may want to charge us import duties, but we just charge them the same. It will cancel itself out. The problem is that if we start arguing reasons for staying, they will shoot us down every time, So that is what we should do. Don't give their ideas the oxygen of publicity. Shoot down their arguments instead.

PM   What about positive reasons for staying? Shouldn't we argue them

Adviser	Well, we could bang on about what a wonderful politicians' club it is, but I don't think the general public would appreciate that. The positives all cost money and the public don't want us to spend money so we have to be careful. I think our argument is so obvious it doesn't need to be vocalised, so we should just wait and see what the beer-swiller and the shagger have to say and shout them down. Destroy their argument. They will have nowhere to go.
PM	True, but we still need to say something positive. What should that be?
Adviser	Why fight it? No one is going to listen to those two buffoons
PM	So what we are saying is, when they come up with a reason to leave, we counter by saying that they are wrong.
Adviser	Yup, that's about the size of it. Walk in the park.
PM	Okay.

Adviser	If we highlight intelligent, well respected remainers and push the idea that it is the 'intelligent' thing to do, that might make people less inclined to argue against
PM	What, tell everyone that the leave supporters are stupid? Isn't that a little dangerous?
Adviser	I wouldn't say it like that. Perhaps just try to slip it in to the conversation and get other people to draw those conclusions.

The meeting ends, and they go on their merry way with a clear strategy that they have no strategy. Now it's the leave campaign leaders who have a similar meeting at around the same time:

Farage	How are we going to convince Johnny public to vote to leave?
BJ	There are very specific areas that they are complaining about. We could target them.
Farage	Okay, let's go through them. But we have to put across a positive message. The 'remain' politicians are just worried about losing their pension plan. The one that consists of

retiring to the life of an MEP with a nice fat expenses package. There isn't much in the way of benefits for the general public. It is purely political, so they won't have much positive to say.

BJ
Okay, so, money. 350 million goes from our coffers into Europe every week. That gets distributed to all the other member states. We get some back but not all.

Farage
Okay, good, 350 million a week going out that won't go out when we leave.

BJ
Not strictly true, th...

Farage
Never mind, we have to keep the message simple. We are talking about Johnny public after all. 350 million going out now. That is 350 a week we save. The NHS needs funding, so we can suggest that this would be a better place to spend that sort of cash.

BJ
We aren't going to plough 350 million a week into the NHS.

Farage
No, of course not! It's just an example, but we keep the message simple. If they start

shouting about it, they will only be helping us get the message out. What next?

BJ   Borders. We'll have more control.

Farage Easy one, that one! We can decide who we allow into our country. We can't control a terrorist threat if people can walk into Europe with little in the way of checks, then be at Liberty to cross our borders and blow us up with impunity.

BJ   We have to be aware that we don't come across as racist. And we have to remember that most Isis incidents have been carried out by people who were born and bred in this country

Farage Keep it simple. We know people are slipping in through asylum loopholes, but we just concentrate on the simple message. Anyway, who in their right mind would think us racist? That would never happen. It's our little secret. Listen, as long as we keep reminding people that we can be better off outside the political union. We can bring them around. It's a difficult sell,

192

and we don't have much chance if the remain campaign has convincing arguments, but we can do this.

So the campaign gets underway. The dreaded Boris bus is wheeled out, proclaiming that we hand over 350 million a week and that we are better off funding the NHS with that sort of money. The remain campaign latch onto this and take the statement literally. They point out that we get most of it back anyway and start suggesting that they are promising would they plough all that money into the NHS. As if any campaign slogan should be taken literally. They latch onto the immigration issue and tell everyone that they are going to exclude people because of the colour of their skin. This is fine by me, if they want to say that, let them say it. But back it up with facts. The campaign by the leavers could have been more honest. It was all positive and extolled the advantages of leaving while not strictly clarifying the details. But the remainers were equally dishonest by suggesting that the leavers were saying things that they weren't, by simply taking campaign slogans literally.

It wasn't just the finances that were used. The Leave campaign treated us to swathes of promises that we would have more control over our laws and that we wouldn't have to kowtow to the whims of Eurocrats. We

193

were going to have control of our borders so that we could control the terrorist threat better. We could control immigration so we could choose who could live here and how many. The message was full of positive phrases to push the idea that their whole campaign was a positive one. One that didn't bear scrutiny, but a positive one nevertheless. If something doesn't bear scrutiny, scrutinise it.

On the other hand, the 'Remainers' were all negative. 'it will be awful if we leave,' 'We will be denied free movement around Europe,' 'We will be isolated', etc. This was the scaremongering side of it. Their other strategy was to ridicule the leavers with reports like 'Remainers have a higher IQ than leavers' and 'leavers are racist.' That is the sort of thing that would get anyone's back up, quite aside from the fact that it was grossly inaccurate. The truth is that I cannot recall one incident where the remain campaign stepped up and extolled the virtues of remaining. They stuck to the negative side of leaving, and this is never going to turn out well. The remainer's complete lack of positivity in their campaign, with not one single vocalised positive reason for remaining, must have been what lost it for them.

In our Brexit scenario, it was very necessary to get proper balance and clearly stated pros and cons on both sides of the argument. Someone decided we were never going to get this. Any psychologist will tell you that there are hundreds of studies about polling and statistics-gathering that show quite clearly that positive messages will win the day. This is clearly what happened in the Brexit' debate'. It also won the day in the USA with Trump. His messages were all almost identical to the Brexit strategy – bigger, better, more stable, stronger, richer. The democrats had the same way of dealing as the remain campaign, negative, negative and yet more negative. Look what happened. I believe there was an experiment some decades ago studying this. They sent interviewers out to get peoples' views on whether to compel young people to do military service upon leaving school. Half of the canvassers were to ask the public if they wanted their sons – it was that long ago that girls were even considered – to be called up and learn discipline, have a sense of structure and try to have a positive impact on the world. This was all positive and encouraging and clearly designed to get people to say yes. The other half were to go out and ask if they wanted their sons to learn to kill people, invade other countries and learn how to get what they want through violence and all that negative stuff. It doesn't take a genius to work out how the study results would present itself.

Everyone has now had their chance to put their side and a people are now ready to have their say. Comedians the

195

length and breadth of the UK are lampooning the leave voters. Newspapers are leaning heavily toward the remain campaign and academics have counted the votes before anyone has had the opportunity to put an X in the box and declared it a victory for the remain campaign. It wasn't. The vote is not exactly decisive, but it went the way of the leave campaign. Many people were saying things like 65 per cent of people didn't vote for Brexit, forgetting that this meant that 68 per cent did not vote to remain, that is over two thirds. Bad argument.

Now, how do the European politicians deal with this? They know that there are rumblings throughout Europe from many quarters. They don't want them to find out that it is easy. The bureaucrats would lose financially every time a richer country leaves. Make no mistake, the only reason they didn't want the UK to leave was the 350 million quid a week that they wouldn't get. I know that the UK got much of this back, and we weren't throwing 350 million down a bottomless pit, but the European political leaders would not have made such a fuss if they weren't losing a substantial chunk of that. So now they have to get around a table to strategize:

Barnier   We need to work out what to do with this Brexit problem.

Macron	Oo cares? Ooo needs les Rosbif anyway?
Barnier	No one, but we do need their cash. We have a nice comfy life here. If we just allow everyone to walk away, this pleasant life will start to become a little prickly. What do we do about it?
Macron	Do what the French do and just shrug your shoulders and say 'Non'. Works for us.
Barnier	Okay, so they are going to come and negotiate trade deals with us.
Macron	Just say Non. Put barriers up. Refuse to even negotiate. Tell them that they need to put certain things in place before we talk to them. Then when they comply, get them to jump through another different hoop.
Barnier	But we still need stuff from Britain. We need to get them to buy our stuff. We need them to take their share of refugees.
Macron	As far as trade, we just publicly say we are not interested but privately continue as we are. We need to keep up the front to discourage other countries from doing the

same thing. As far as refugees are concerned. We just continue doing what we always have. Make it as uncomfortable as possible for them in France, so they go to any lengths to get away from us. Keep them on the North coast so that their only escape is to the UK. South Coast won't do, the only option would be back from whence they came. They aren't going back if they have made this much effort to get away.

Barnier   That would be like they are escaping France, not their country of origin. Would it not be a little risky to have them seeking asylum from France?

Macron   The language of diplomacy without being diplomatic is a skill set in which the French excel

Barnier   What about importing British goods?

Macron   We ignore their fishing limits. Both the geographic ones and the quantities. Then we just drown them in bureaucracy for anything or anyone coming into Europe.

Barnier	Belgians are particularly skilled at bureaucracy. I think we can handle that. We can spend days going over the briefest of documents and then reject a whole load of others because they have forgotten to use an upper case at the beginning of a proper noun on that one piece of paper. So, our strategy is to make life as difficult as possible. We set up a negotiating channel and then refuse to negotiate. We continue to trade but publicly say we aren't and make it difficult for them to export into Europe.
Macron	Exactly
Barnier	So we dictate terms instead of negotiating them
Macron	I'm going to enjoy this.

We now, in the year 2023, appear to be in a position where people are travelling to Europe with relative ease. The COVID pandemic has put a spanner into the works, but it seems to be working okay. I do have an issue with post, though. I sent packages to Europe. Pre-Brexit, it was fine. It isn't now. I find that the recipients of my parcels have to pay to retrieve them in some European countries. They cite import duties, admin and such like but are charging ten times the value of the package. I can send things to anywhere in the world. The only place where it gets held up is Europe and South Africa. The South African issue is one of incompetence, but the European one is not. I have even had to send a package bound for Denmark via Thailand to avoid the ludicrous bureaucracy. How bad is that! Many people seek to defend this, saying that bureaucratic processes have to be maintained if you are outside their sphere of influence. That argument would be fine if it were the same for every other country in the world. Why would there be less bureaucracy in a package from Thailand? Since then, I actually posted a package in Austria to go to Denmark. It took over three weeks to get to its destination. I could have got a schoolboy to kick it down the road all the way quicker.

In conclusion, I am European. My DNA tells me that I am English to the core. I have a little bit of 'North European', but my name originates from the northeast coast of England, which is where the Vikings landed, so it is to be expected. I always get along with our European brethren, and I enjoy visiting the different countries in the union. Each country is distinctly different – mainly in a good way – and everyone seems to want it that way. I don't think a single Europe under one government would work at this point. We all have different languages, different ways of dealing with issues and different priorities. There is, whether we like it or not, a national pride in each country, so you would probably find that if there were one elected government for Europe, each country would vote for their own candidate. That means the most populous country would always have the leader they want, and no one else will. Just my opinion. We don't need a European parliament while we have separate countries all with their own ones, and a single Europe under one parliament wouldn't work under current conditions. That is just politics for politics' sake. But we do need a Europe that works together. This would be achieved by sensible politicians (an oxymoron if ever there was one) being sensible with each other. Don't hold your breath.

DRUGS

I have now ranted about the media and politics. Both of these have one main thing in common in my life. That is that I have no experience of either and little knowledge of how they work. I, therefore, have no real basis on which to pass an opinion. With that in mind, I am now going to delve into the dark nether world of drugs. Legal and illegal. I have no experience in the industry whatsoever. I don't use pharmaceuticals much as a rule, and I have never worked in the industry. Nor have I ever knowingly used illegal narcotics. They never interested me. I have dealt with the consequences of addiction in other people in my working life, but only the fallout. The subject does interest me, and I believe that politicians are the cause of much of what has happened over the last 80-plus years.

Pharma

I'm not a worrier, but I do worry about our pharmaceutical companies worldwide. These are companies that are tasked with finding medical remedies for all of our maladies. Someone has to do it, and who else is more qualified than a company that employs a bucket load of chemists, researchers and other scientists?

The answer to that question is, quite obviously, none. The problem does not come with who is doing the investigations; it is how and why they are being done. A good friend of mine who is qualified to pass an opinion, as he and his wife hold doctorates and she is employed in the area of medical exploration into pharmaceuticals, stated that he got annoyed when he heard people suggesting that these companies had no integrity and that their primary function was to look after their shareholders. He called it conspiracy theories and dismissed them. I was unable to engage in the conversation at the time, but I will remedy that now.

The issue is not one of conspiracy theories; it is one of business. The fact is that all pharmaceutical companies are privately owned, profit-making businesses. This means that not only are their bosses insisting that they turn a profit, but they want as healthy a profit as they can get. So, consider this completely hypothetical scenario. A large pharmaceutical company is given a contract to come up with a medical remedy for Alzheimer's disease. Now we know the causes of Alzheimer's disease. The way I understand it from my layman's point of view is that the brain is constantly dealing with protein build-up. If there is too much of a build-up, the synapses start being blocked. In order to tackle this, it produces a substance similar to insulin. This substance breaks down the protein deposits and keeps the brain functioning. In Alzheimer's patients, this insulin-type substance is not being produced in sufficient quantities. This causes a build-up of protein deposits, which, in turn, causes blockages causing the brain's responses to be diminished. It would then seem to me that, when looking for cures, one should start with this issue and ask the question, 'How do we get the brain to start producing this chemical? They can all introduce synthetic chemicals that try to simulate or emulate it, but the most effective way is to get the brain to do it for itself.

The pharmaceutical company sends its intrepid chemists off to come up with something. Six months later, they troop back into the office with three solutions. One should always give your boss three options and subtly guide their decision-makers towards the one that is favoured. The three options are as follows: Euthanasia (probably not something they would debate too long and hard). Then we have one remedy that deals with the symptoms of Alzheimer's but cannot cure it. It is cheap to produce and can be sold to the NHS cheaply so that the end user would have to pay no more than a few pounds per tablet. They would be on the medication for the rest of their lives, but it would be a healthier, more coherent life. There would also be a steady income for the company. The last option is a miracle cure! They have discovered how to get the brain stimulated into producing the missing chemical. This

204

would deal with the problem at a stroke (not a stroke in the medical sense) and would reverse the disease. I believe that research has shown that this disease can be reversed, so this hypothetical scenario is not compromised. The downside for the customer is that it is prohibitively expensive, and the upside is that they would be cured, so unlike the first one, they wouldn't be forking out for the cost of the medication the rest of their days.

Any shareholder, stakeholder, director of a profit-chasing company, or anyone else looking at these two options would conclude that the second option would pay for itself, but the patient would only need one dose. The first option would give them a guaranteed income, albeit slow and steady. What leader of a profit-making enterprise would opt for the second one? They are not there to cure people. If they did that every time, they would put themselves out of business. Far better the first option. It's an easy sell to the politicians. Just mention how much the one costs, as opposed to the other. Deftly avoid the issue that the government would be paying more in the long run – politicians don't do 'long run,' five years maximum in the UK is as futuristic as they get – and concentrate on short-term savings. All this does not, in my view, fall into the conspiracy theory category, just the money-making one.

On paper, this situation is easy to sort out. Put all pharmaceutical companies under the control of governments. In the UK, they have to pay out for the medicines anyway so that they would save money in a short period of time. The companies could then be non-profit, making concerns. This would mean that the governments of countries without the NHS or similar could charge less for the medications, which means more people could have access to the said medication.

Easy on paper. One would have to persuade countries like America, who seem to believe that anything that helps the less well-off is the work of the devil – or worse, bordering on communism. A pharmaceutical industry that doesn't chase profits has to be better than what we have now. I am not an advocate of nationalising industry. Healthy competition is a good thing. There are, however, plenty of areas where competition isn't required and, in the case of pharmaceutical companies, is detrimental to the general health and well-being of all. Nor do I believe that the industry would become less efficient. We are dealing primarily with academics whose whole ethos is finding stuff out. That is their motive, not making millions for company directors who wouldn't know one end of a test tube from another but could give you chapter and verse about balance sheets.

Narcotics

There are few people in the world who are not affected in one way or another by the issue of illegalised drugs. Whether it be countries like Afghanistan and Columbia, which have economies that rely to a lesser or greater degree on drug revenue, countries like some Caribbean islands and the Florida Keys that are staging posts for the import/export industry or countries like the USA and the countries in Europe that deal with the results of addictions, let us not kid ourselves that there isn't a problem. Some of the largest criminal organisations committing some of the most heinous crimes and destroying countless lives are involved. We shouldn't forget that, but we can look at how to deal with it. To do this, we have to consider how the problem started. In my eyes, the problem was not the drugs; it was how the people in positions of responsibility dealt with them. It wasn't much more than a hundred years ago that little or no legislation existed to control "social" drugs – that is to say drugs that are not prescribed for medicinal purposes. I am not saying that there were no issues. Opium dens with people hopelessly addicted to the stuff were in existence all over Europe, Asia and probably the USA. It just wasn't at the epidemic proportions that it has grown to. And the spark that lit this particular fuse, I believe, was legislation to restrict the possession and sales of it.

Looking at the history, we know that heroin was a substance that was developed specifically for medical purposes. It was properly patented and sold to the medical industry. The problem was that they were aware of its addictive qualities. This, in itself, is not the issue. The issue is that, at my most generous, I can believe that the medical industry ignored that fact and allowed their patients to become addicted without bothering with any kind of exit plan. At worst – and not beyond belief – is the idea that some instances were deliberate. In the countries where there is no real free medical service, people rely upon medical insurance. This means that doctors get paid every time they see a patient, and they make a profit from providing medication. The pharmaceutical companies have been known to encourage doctors to medicate more heavily, thereby increasing everyone's profits. The more people were put on this new Heroin medicine, the more they relied on it, the more it became less effective, so that more was needed for the same effect.

The American government noticed all this and realised that a serious problem was developing. What do they do about it? Ban it outright. There and then. That is all very well, but those people who are now hopelessly addicted to it as a direct result of their doctors providing it to them suddenly had their supplies cut off. Anyone with an ounce of common sense can see that someone who needs this stuff and who is told that their legitimate supply lines no longer exist will not just shrug their shoulders and say, 'Oh well, never mind, I'll just have to take up knitting instead.' No, they are going to find other ways of getting hold of it.

All of this is because some doctors were more interested in their balance sheets than their patients' health. And exacerbated by the intransigence of politicians who only want to make it look like they are doing something to solve a problem, only to pass the results of their bad decisions to the next incumbent.

Another part of this issue is that when they banned heroin, they didn't stick to that substance alone. They lumped together all substances that they considered harmful or in roughly the same category and banned the lot. So cocaine, which is not as addictive or harmful as cut heroin when taken on its own, falls into the same category. Cannabis, which has some disadvantages but again is not as addictive, if it is at all, is also put into the catch-all that people have come to refer to as 'drugs'. I see no reason why governments can't be selective when dealing with this issue. We have an obvious problem with crack cocaine, which is a more intense version of coke and very much addictive. This stuff is causing massive problems because people will do anything to get their hands on it. Methamphetamine is even worse from the addictive qualities and the physical damage it does, not to mention the unscrupulous peddlers of these substances. These are a world away from a bunch of hippies passing around a joint.

As a result of the legislative controls placed on these substances, which quickly spread to other parts of the world, the pharmaceutical companies could no longer supply it, but they knew there was a demand, so they managed to get the stuff out there to less-than-honest people who are not constrained by inconvenient laws. Let's face it, whether or not heroin was patented, once it became illegal, the patent wasn't worth the paper it was printed on. These outsiders can now charge what they like, and they can also mix it with cheaper stuff to make their profit margins grow. Heroin now goes from being a useful, if somewhat addictive, medicine to a substance that could and did contain all sorts of harmful crap. This made it dangerous to the health of the user but no less addictive. The users become enslaved by it metaphorically but also physically in some cases. Many ended up losing their jobs as they could no longer function and they took to crime to feed their habit. In the meantime, the suppliers are getting richer and ensuring more and more people are ensnared by it. They tended to target the poorer communities, telling them that they can have relief from the drudgery of their lives, only to find that, before long, they are either addicted or a part of the supply chain or both, as was often the case.

Do we legalise it? Well we haven't stopped it so we may as well. At least then we can control quality, tax it and stop, or at least inhibit the criminal gangs that pray on the people to become enslaved by it. The powers that be have no problem with keeping tobacco and alcohol legal, they are also addictive and injurious to health.

Cannabis

It has been interesting over the past few years to watch the attitude of people in different areas deal with the issue of cannabis. Does it have a medical application? If so, what is it, and what are the downsides? How do we make money out of it? How do we legalise it without having to admit we were mistaken in illegalising it in the first place?

For decades we have been told that cannabis has great remedial qualities. No one was really able or willing to quantify what these qualities were. This allowed the medical profession, and in particular, the pharmaceutical

211

companies, to dismiss all mention of cannabis as the only available evidence was 'anecdotal evidence' and, as such, not enough to use by the medical profession. This attitude really winds me up because any scientist worthy of being called that, should be seeing that the 'anecdotal evidence' of which there is an embarrassment of riches, all seems to point in the same direction. If that is the case, take this anecdotal evidence, study it, and come up with empirical evidence either way. Surely that should be the default position of any scientist.

I am aware that cannabis has had adverse psychological effects on people. It seems that the majority of these unfortunate people are those who used too much and too strong when they were very young and their brains were still developing. We know that there are mental hospitals full of people with what has been described to me as 'drug-induced psychoses.' These seem to be people who were using the very strong 'skunk' and abusing it at a young age. Now we are all aware that alcohol and drugs damage brain cells. But what does that mean? A medical friend described to me what happens when the body renews cells. He used photocopying as a way to demonstrate his point. In essence, cells renew by dividing. Every element of the cell splits in two then the cell splits sharing the split particles equally between the two halves. This allows old cells to die off and be replaced. Like

212

photocopying, it can only reproduce the information it has. If one redacts a page and copies that page, then discards the original. All you are left with is the redaction, and that other blanked-out information is lost. If you break an arm, a doctor can reset it. If you break an arm and lose the section that is broken so that it is irretrievable, no doctor in the world is going to be able to regrow that arm. In the same way, if our cells are damaged when they divide, they can't reproduce what they haven't got so they have to produce the redacted version. When the healthy cells then get old and die off, that information is lost. So, if my understanding is correct, if the substances we take as a youngster damage vital information contained in our cells, then that information could be lost forever. If the information being lost is things dealing with your mental well-being, then that is going to be lost. There are two main active ingredients in cannabis. CBD oils and THC oils. The THCs are the psycho-active oils. If it is going to affect brain function, then it stands to reason that young, developing brains are at risk of being permanently damaged. Especially if it irreversibly inhibits development.

This is not to say if you have a spliff, you will descend into a psychotic downward spiral out of which you will never emerge, but for some developing brains, abuse could be a causal factor.

Big Pharma has been fighting the introduction of THCs and CBD oils for decades. They are clearly worried that their medication isn't going to sell if this stuff is a miracle cure for all our ailments. They did the same with vitamins. There was a period where they had people believing that you could overdose on some vitamins and cause serious long-term harm. We had a recommended daily intake so as not to fall foul of this. and health warnings on bottles. There was a study that showed that not only did vitamin C, for example, pose no risk, but there were significant benefits when 250 times the RDI was taken intravenously and absolutely no negative side effects. So maybe it was just that they hadn't managed to get all their ducks in a row with the active chemicals in cannabis, and small, independent industries managed initially to corner the market. These huge juggernauts of organisations were slow to react. While they have been arguing against its introduction, they have been busy in the background remedying this oversight. They have become remarkably quiet in recent years. A cynic may suggest that it is because they are now producing the stuff and are squeezing the little guy out of the market. Mainstream advertising has started happening. I know of some who have started farming cannabis under licence. They tell me that the controls are manic. They can't even plant the stuff until they have a guaranteed buyer for the whole crop. Security is paramount. We can't have young hippies coming to help themselves whenever they please. How would the government get taxes that way? This obviously means that only large Pharma can commit the sort of sums that can handle these quantities and small independents will be side-lined.

It looks like all the legal farms will have to be sponsored by large pharmaceuticals. To me, this just says that the pharmaceutical lobbyists have managed to convince the politicians to allow production, but only in a way that is beneficial to them. So small independents are either going to disappear or they will reappear underground. They can still make a decent living. They can't be prosecuted for selling CBD oil under any drug related legislation, only growing the plant that produces it. I cannot say that I would be surprised if the product coming out of these smaller concerns will be better than the big, profit-making, balance sheet obsessed multicorporate organisations.

The criminal system in the UK is not exactly awash with cannabis offenders anymore. A much more liberal attitude by police is being taken, and users seldom find themselves muttering apologies to magistrates for having a spliff up their sleeve. Unless, of course, they are there for other more serious issues as well, and the cannabis was just found in the course of an investigation. Most governments around the world seem to be keen to shed themselves of laws surrounding this relatively mild drug. I don' think it is difficult to separate it from the more harmful drugs. I think they just need to recognise that if it grows naturally, like cannabis and magic mushrooms, then leave the legislation alone. If they can control quality – in the same way as they control food quality, for example – and prevent vulnerable people from permanently damaging their brains while allowing adults to use it, so much the better. And if they can tax it...

Cannabis Factories

One of the most damaging things about the cannabis industry is something that most people know little or nothing about. Before I start, while I recognise that there may be a little stereotyping, I am in no way saying that all these people are of the same racial profile, nor am I saying that any more than a few individuals from that part of the world are doing all of this, I can't escape the fact that I personally never came across this type of scenario where anyone other than Chinese and Vietnamese people were involved.

Illegal cannabis factories are popping up everywhere. We know this because it takes a lot of extra energy to grow the stuff in the UK. Helicopters with heat sensitive cameras say that there are so many private houses that have heat signatures off the scale – indicating very high energy use and therefore the likely presence of hydroponics used in the growing of cannabis – that the police just don't have the resources to stop it. Why bother I hear you ask. Well, let me tell you a story. While this all may not be true in all cases, it is a very common theme. What happens is that a seemingly respectable, predominantly Chinese couple will go to an estate agent asking for a rental for a limited period, three months or so. It needs to be a relatively large premises with loft space. They will have identification documents that would bear close scrutiny but would be entirely false. They then pay for the entire rental period in cash up front. This sounds like a great deal for the landlord, but it isn't. They then move in and rip out all the fixtures and fittings and furniture and dump it all. Where they can, they divert electricity from elsewhere so they have no bills to pay, and the next-door neighbour will get a massive shock three months after they have flown the coop. They then use all the available space including the loft area and put hydroponic equipment in. they plant the seeds then insert a lacky who is normally a Vietnamese refugee or similar. They threaten the family of their chosen lacky then disappear returning every so often to check on their product. He would have to live there in the bathroom with a gas camping cooker and a few blankets because all other space is full of equipment. If the place is discovered by the authorities, the poor lacky is arrested and knows nothing about the operation. The people gaining the benefit are untraceable as they would have given false details which would not have been checked closely because the landlord has already been paid so he doesn't have to worry. They lose a few thousand pounds and a cannabis crop, but they have dozens more dotted about. When the crop is ready, if they haven't been discovered, the crop is harvested, loaded up and they all disappear into the ether, never to be seen again leaving all the equipment behind for someone else to deal with. The house for which the landlord will have received ten thousand pounds or whatever the deal was, will have to be refurnished, rewired, replumbed and rebuilt entirely at costs of many tens of thousands of pounds and the lacky is just abandoned to find his own way back to his family or used in another project somewhere else in the country. So when you are sucking on your spliff, just consider who else is being harmed by the industry. For those who are wagging their righteous fingers right now, consider that legalisation would probably wipe this whole system out at a stroke.

There are so many other products on the market today. The 60s had weed and LSD, since then MDMA, speed, methamphet. All sorts of uppers and downers. The horse tranquilliser ketamine is in common use. Date rape drugs are ever present although interestingly, there has never been a successful prosecution off the back of these drugs. I know it has not been for want of trying. Unfortunately, the only way one can prove it is to find the evidence in blood samples from the victim. When I left the service, the police had never had a positive hit from a lab submission looking for date rape drugs and so could never use it as part of the evidence. We know it's out there, we just can't nail it down. It was suggested at one point that the stuff left your system within 24 hours and this was why we couldn't nail it. I have since been told of a scientist who used himself as a guinea pig to test this theory. He took the stuff then tested himself regularly until there was no traces left in his system. I believe he was still finding traces five days later. I couldn't say how accurate this anecdote is, but I can see someone doing this and I don't see why they would lie about the results. I suppose it doesn't help when a young lady goes out and drinks her own body weight in alcohol then insists that one of the half dozen shots, the two bottles of wine or the countless beers she had must have been spiked. It couldn't possibly be that she was drunk. I'm not saying that young ladies shouldn't get drunk, nor am I saying it is the lady's fault for being drunk. The blame will always be on the attacker, not the target. All I am saying is that if one is drunk, then admit it and don't let

219

the police spend time effort and money researching something that they will never find.

In conclusion to this I will say that, as a young man I was very much against drug abuse. I would avoid contact and if I thought it was anywhere near me, I would not be happy. I think this attitude has served me well in the long term but it meant that I remained ignorant of the entire subject for the first half of my life. I believe that my main objection was the fact that it was illegal. This is odd because I have never been a rules-is-rules kind of a guy. I also believe it is the wrong reason to be so fervently against something. If you were walking down the road minding your own business, whistling a happy tune when you come across a vehicle with its engine running and no one anywhere near the car. If you are partial to stealing cars, you would probably take it. If, like me, you are not so inclined, the first thing to come into your mind would not be, 'would I get away with it if I drove off now?' It would probably be closer to, "That's a bit dumb, anyone could nick that car.' But you would never consider that 'anyone' to be yourself. And it wouldn't be because it is against the law. It would be because you don't think that stealing is a good thing. The same should go for drugs. Don't be against it purely because it is against the law. We can see how damaging the law has been on this subject. Look at the bigger picture and be against it for more sensible reasons.

WOKISM

I'm not woke. I don't like people who are. They seem to spend their lives trying not to offend and, in so doing, end up offending someone else for a different reason, normally as a result of ignorance. It is my belief that if you are not out to offend by what you are saying, if someone decides to be offended, there is normally a reasonable explanation that would clear the air. A simple enquiry, even just saying, 'I don't think that is a nice thing to say', would elicit an explanation that would clarify. Try it instead of walking away in a huff and complaining to a friend who was nowhere near at the time and can offer no views on the incident. Or, even worse accuse the person of whatever 'ism' you think they have breached then walk away before making sure that there isn't a good explanation. It may cause you to re-evaluate your own views.

I do not believe one can be 'accidentally racist'. Someone who is making racist statements is doing so because they believe that the race against whom they are being offensive is in some way inferior or nasty or something else that is derogatory to their senses. There is nothing accidental about that. Equally if one uses language that is dated, in a way that is clearly not meant to be insulting, they are just old fashioned, not racist. As an example, there was an incident in British politics where a white female MP, while verbally attacking online trolls, stated that women, and 'coloured women in particular', were more vulnerable to this rather nasty and cowardly form of attack. One black female who was in the opposition party, made a hue and cry about her opposite number's use of language and wanted her to resign her position. Apparently, the word 'coloured' is somehow offensive, regardless of the context. What she and her supporters had done was to ignore the message – trolls are nasty and cowardly, and some people were more vulnerable than others – and concentrate entirely on what was nothing more than an out-of-fashion way of referring to black people. There was nothing derogatory about what she said. In fact, it was quite supportive, if a little patronising. The only explanation that I can come up with is that the complainants were just trying to make political capital by invoking wokism.

My personal view was that race had little, if anything, to do with the commentary and could have been left out completely. Many MPs are subject to this trolling phenomenon. I can believe that women can be more prone to the nastiness. I hear of people threatening rape and all sorts. These are almost always empty threats, but it must still be upsetting. I don't see how ethnic minorities would be more threatened by this than anyone else. I can see that racist outbursts cannot be pleasant, I certainly haven't liked it when it has been aimed at me, but are they worse than rape threats? The sceptic in me thinks that the person making the political gaff was trying to be woke and failing. The complainant was trying to gain political points and failing. It would be nice if these idiots (and I refer to the trolls and both politicians alike) just desisted in their chosen path. I cannot imagine how screwed up someone's mind has to be to take pleasure in upsetting people they don't know. They don't even get to see the results of their idiocy because they live in front of a computer screen.

I have little time for those who believe that positive discrimination is a good thing. It isn't, it is just racism or sexism or any other ism wrapped up and presented in a new way to appease politicians. Just think about the language. As in mathematics, positive times positive equals positive. Negative times negative equals positive and negative times positive is always negative. When we use the word 'discrimination', we aren't talking about one's discriminating tastes in garden furniture, we are talking about differentiating between people through race, gender, religion, sexual orientation and so forth. So discrimination in this context is negative. 'Positive', you may be surprised to learn, is positive. Put them together and it is linguistically negative. It essentially says that the speaker is in favour of discrimination. We can't even use the excuse that it is discrimination in a positive way, because if you discriminate in favour of someone on the grounds of race, you have to logically discriminate against another person on the same grounds. The fact that the person receiving the benefit of the 'positive discrimination' belongs to a minority group makes no difference. The person advocating for this type of discrimination would therefore be a racist by definition.

The big problem comes when people don't want to confront the question head-on. We end up with bad decisions from decision makers who are scared of their own shadows. This allows for the issues to be used by unscrupulous people in order to try to weaponise the circumstances.

There was an openly gay senior police officer who went on to campaign for a major political position. Thankfully this failed dismally; I didn't like him one bit. It was nothing to do with his sexuality, which he had no trouble in telling everyone about. It was the underlying message that I didn't like. I am told of a story that he would go into the police canteen, plonk himself down at a random table with a load of people enjoying their refreshment break and start talking about his wild sexual romps from the night before. I cannot remember any time that I sat at a canteen table and described in lurid detail my sexual activities from the night before or any other night. Nor can I remember ever having to endure anything more than passing comments on this subject. And I was a man who was a detective in the sexual offences department of the Met Police for a significant chunk of my service. This was an office where the language was blue from the moment you walked in in the morning to the moment you went home. Canteens tend to have an unspoken etiquette. People tend to eat with members of their team or people who they have befriended. It isn't tribal or anything, and I imagine every work canteen in the world works the same. So, someone from outside your immediate group who just randomly plonks themselves down is always going to be a little odd. Going into those sorts of details with people you don't know is definitely not on. Why on earth did he think that anyone would be interested in his sexual activities? I think the answer is simple. He was challenging people to say anything or make any gestures that would give him ammunition in the future. Anyone who walked away without finishing their meal. Anyone who changed tables for no apparent reason. Anyone who made any sort of comment about what he was saying could have been a target for his political ambitions to their detriment. Why else do it? He was essentially trying to weaponise his sexuality. I don't believe that he got anywhere. Whatever you may think of coppers, they are a savvy bunch and won't fall for rubbish like that.

I remember another story involving two 4-year-old kids, one black and one white, playing in a play group that had been set up within a supermarket complex for harassed parents to be able to do the grocery shopping while someone else looked after the kids. The details of the story have faded somewhat, but essentially one boy told the other kid that he looked like a monkey. I don't know if they were arguing, fighting over a toy, or playing nicely and joking around. The upshot was that the parent was called in immediately, and the boy was banned from the playgroup. I don't like racial insults by anyone against anyone, but 4-year-old boys? Please! This was purely a visual taunt by a boy who would not have understood the concept of race. As a police officer, I have tried to get descriptions from kids older than that, and, as a general rule, skin colour is not even thought of. Asking a child what colour a person's skin is, was a challenge. 'Skin coloured' is about all you would get. It is only when one gets corrupted by the opinions of the outside world as we grow up and get a political conscience (or lack thereof) that these things become more significant. To brand a 4-year-old boy as a racist is wokism at its worst. By all means, use the incident to teach a lesson. Perhaps even investigate to make sure the parents aren't wronguns. Don't just assume the worst. The parents must have been beside themselves if they were even remotely decent.

Entertainment industry

What is acting? It is storytelling using actions. It is pretending to be someone or something that you are not in order to tell your story. I was listening to the radio one day. It was a comedy channel, and Stephen Fry was one of the panellists. During the course of the show, the host asked who Mr Fry thought should act his character if there was ever a biopic made of his life. This is a tricky question to answer because if he came across too enthusiastic, then he would appear shallow. If he tried to avoid the question, it would be false humility. I think he handled it well – right up until he started questioning whether it would have to be a gay actor because he is a gay man. Why? Why do gay parts require gay men? If you took that line of thought to its logical conclusion, then surely all straight parts should be played by straight people. I think the film industry may struggle if that was ever a thing. Why does he believe that a straight man would not do as good a job as a gay man? They would, after all, be pretending to be Stephen Fry, so why can't they pretend to be gay? They are not vicariously living his life for him in every detail.

It goes further than this. I have heard on several occasions people questioning why a white actor was playing the role normally played by a black person. This complaint seemed to have broad support, and I got to thinking about this.

Denzel Washington, a particularly good black American actor, recently played Macbeth, a famously white role. No one batted an eyelid. And why would they? He is a very good actor, and he would have done a good job of it, I'm sure. What does it matter what colour his skin is? I have heard some Americans postulating that Shakespeare in an American accent sounds wrong, but that is just their point of view and a different discussion. But it has to go both ways. Why would it not? It is still acting. It is still pretending. The actors are still just telling a story. The story doesn't change just because someone looks or sounds a little different. Let's just allow people to express themselves in whatever way they want.

So here is a suggested solution. Write a play that involves men and women; people from various racial profiles; people with varying sexual preferences; people with varying disabilities. Then audition a load of people with all these differences and choose a cast that reflects the play itself. Then, either deliberately cast them as something other than the obvious, (preferred option), or, for each performance, just pull names out of a hat for each role so that you could get anyone playing any role (this, I would suggest, would be quite difficult as the entire cast would have to know every character and all the lines). Do not change their appearance in any way. Black people could be playing white roles, white people playing oriental people.

229

Straight Asian men playing gay black females. Just a complete mishmash. I would let the audience in on the idea from the get-go so that their ideas are challenged. I think it would be a great social experiment. I imagine the audience would struggle at first but, by the end, would have forgotten about the concept and, if the play is any good, would be sitting back and enjoying the entertainment.

Cancel Culture

Now I get controversial. I don't think it's controversial, but the woke world is getting its knickers in a twist about it. JK Rowling got into a spot of bother with this for just being honest and obvious. This is the idea of transgender people and how we address them. Someone referred to a 'person with a womb', and Ms Rowling said something to the effect of, 'We have a word for that in English, "woman"'. For this, the cancel culture brigade came out in force. She was ridiculed. There was a vicious campaign against her. She had a book out that was being made into a film, and the producers wanted to remove her name from the credits. All for stating the obvious.

I am aware that there are people out there who have physical signs of the opposite sex within their bodies. Some women have prostates – although the overwhelming majority are inactive – some men have signs of ovaries. These cases are very rare, so much so that they can't be easily expressed in percentages. This means that, as near as makes no difference, gender is binary. When the word 'man' is preceded by 'the', or is quantified in some way, it becomes gender specific and therefore denotes the male of the species, but historically, the word was used to describe the species as a whole, the word 'she' is a very late addition to the OED. Therefore 'the man', 'a man', 'one man' and 'postman' relate to gender and statements like 'when man first walked the earth' and 'Mankind is the dominant species on earth' does not. This is referring to the entire species, which is divided in two by those who have a womb – wo(mb)man – and those who don't. So, when JK Rowling says that there is a word for a person with a womb, she is being etymologically and scientifically correct. Whether or not she has views on the fact of transsexuality is something I do not know and is none of my business, although I am sure her views are well-formed and reasonable.

I have no problem with people expressing themselves in whatever way they want. If people want me to refer to them and to treat them as a spotted hyena, I am happy to comply. Just don't expect me to think of them as a spotted hyena because they just are not. Of course, if you are going down that road and have decided to live on a diet of raw, discarded bones as hyenas are wont to do, you also need to remember that your digestive system may not have received the email about your species realignment. I do have a problem with people going through irreversible procedures in their early developing years. Their bodies and hormones are still trying to get used to who they are. They need to grow into themselves and be comfortable with whatever identity they want before taking drastic action. The idea that some schools are putting kids through alternative gender therapies without the parents' knowledge is, in my opinion, criminal negligence. There are people who will come to a point in their lives when they feel that this procedure is required for their own physical and mental health. Puberty is not that time. Your body is all over the place. Hormones are changing the signals that your brain is receiving, and confusion reigns. Once all this settles down is the time when therapy and slow transition should be started if you still feel that this is the only route for you. Always remember that you will never be a fully functioning member of your new gender. People transitioning to female will never be able to conceive naturally, they'll never menstruate and they'll never drive me insane with their female logic.

If someone has decided to go through the procedure and go under the knife, I have no issues, crack on, do what you need to do. Please tell me how you want me to refer to you and I will be happy to comply. I have, in my life as a detective in the Sexual offence department, used two statements that sound like oxymorons: 'His vagina' and 'her penis'. One particular incident I am thinking about was one of two transgender people of opposite sexes getting into a serious dispute that involved rape and sexual assault allegations. I had no trouble in dealing with them. The prison system did, though, as they were both 'pre-op' and so didn't know where to put them.

Live your life how you want to live it and embrace it. Just remember that from a scientific point of view, from a physiological point of view and from a molecular point of view, you are and always will be the gender you were born with. If a doctor was to take a sample of your bodily tissue and, without knowing anything about you, is told to determine gender just from the tissue, that doctor should be able to do so, and it will be down to X and Y chromosomes that you have from birth and cannot be altered.

I read with some glee recently that this 'cancel culture' that the writer correctly described as 'censorship' by our woke community is failing and looking like it will be binned. I cannot wait. The article posited the idea that several people have fallen foul of this wokism. Figures suggest that J K Rowling, despite her spat with the woke brigade, has six of the ten most borrowed books in libraries, including the top four positions, and the games that have been developed off the back of her writings are outselling everything. I say this is a victory over this ill-conceived censorship. Mr Roald Dahl, it seems, should have had the sensibilities of the 21st-century youth when he wrote his worldwide best-selling children's books. To this end, a bunch of half-wits (not very woke) have decided to rewrite his novels to suit a modern audience. I have read that these people have listened to the well-directed criticism of their policies and have relented. They will now put out both versions, the PC one and the original. I have no doubt that the original will outsell the other one by a march.

I say to these people that one cannot expunge history or change it to make it sound more palatable. These authors were best-sellers for a reason. Leave their writing alone. People need to know how people thought in those days. We need to experience the wonderful imagination of the writers that have brought pleasure to millions. I can't imagine anyone has grown up mentally damaged as a result of being read The Big Friendly Giant as a bedtime story. Strangely, no one has suggested censoring

Shakespeare or Dickens, and their writing was as far from PC as one could even imagine in today's world.

Dancing

Dancing, now there is a thing. Wokism within the dancing world? Is that possible? Yep, it certainly is, with knobs on. I am referring to Morris dancing mainly – although I'm sure it happens throughout – and some of the ill-considered opinions around this art form. I provide musical accompaniment for people to express this particular art form, so I have been immersed in this quirky world for a few years now. I am by no means an expert in all things Morris, but I have learnt some stuff.

A brief history lesson. There are nine different styles of Morris dancing (if you include highland dancing and Irish dancing, which all come from the same base) based on where they originate. The men in white shirts, hankies and bells are performing the form that originated from the Cotswold area of England; the clog dancers are from Northwest England; Molly dancers are from the fens in the east; sword dancers are from the north and Border dancers are from the Welsh/English borders and several other offshoots. It is the Border Morris style to which I will be referring as they have been singled out as 'blacking up', and this is seen as highly inappropriate and racist. I can say right here and right now that there are no negative racial connotations in their blacking up and that I believe the word Morris may well have come about as a direct result of this face-daubing habit, not the other way around. The word Moresco – which I believe means little Moors – when used to refer to this dance form, was first mentioned in the 15th century. This does not for one moment suggest that dancing on this island started at that point. There will have been dancing for millennia prior to this.

The point is that the word first came to light in writing at that time, so the question is why. The theories for the etymology of the word is well worn. On one side, an old Celtic word for dance was a word very similar to Morris, and it is believed to have morphed into its current spelling. This doesn't explain why the word wasn't used prior to the 15th century, so I question this theory. The other theory is that it is from the word Moresco – little Moor. Protestantism had been gaining momentum in Europe at this time, and they thought this an ideal opportunity to spread their version of christianity. Catholics weren't so keen, so religious turmoil was the way of things to come for the next few centuries. The Catholics, who were quite forgiving, liked to celebrate their faith but insisted that people lived by their rules, even if the rule makers didn't. They did not want anyone outside the church to be able to read. They grudgingly accepted that the aristocracy, doctors and Lawyers needed to read, but they kept everything strictly in Latin so that they had autonomy over everyone. It was for the church to tell people what 'god' wanted them to know. It was for them to interpret the word of god, not mere mortals, and certainly not the peasantry. Don't even mention women. As long as the people threw loads of cash at them, everyone's souls would be saved.

Protestants, on the other hand, felt that the bible needed no interpretation. Although their interpretation of the bible had been around for many years, if not centuries, they had only gained a firm foothold in the UK after Henry VIII sacked the Pope and became head of the new English church. He didn't particularly like the puritanical ways of Protestantism; he preferred the catholic ways. He just didn't want to be dictated to by an Italian bloke who he had never met. As far as the protestants were concerned, if it was written, it was fact. There was no interpretation required. So they wanted everyone to read, be they women, men, children, rich or poor. They wanted them only to read the bible, think the bible, talk the bible, and breathe the bible. They didn't want anyone to celebrate. They didn't want anyone to show any joy or wealth, just live and breathe their god. Theatres were banned, and dancing was considered to be communicating with satan himself. Your day should consist of waking up, pray. Have breakfast, pray. Go to work, pray. If you got any kind of lunch break, pray. Go to church after work, pray. Have dinner, pray. Go to bed and pray. Any days off work should be spent in church. Poverty was rife at this time. Wealthy landowners would work their workers to the bone for no more than basic rations and a shelter over their heads. Many people did other things to make extra money to eat and drink. One of these things was dancing. But you had to be careful. If you get caught, you could be burnt alive for communing with the antichrist. So they disguised themselves. They wore their jackets inside out and decorated them so they all looked similar (We call these 'tatter jackets'). They wore similar hats, and they used whatever they had to hand to smear their faces to disguise their features. Colliers would use coal; farm workers would use the soil, blacksmiths, the soot from their fires. If they were caught, they could run off, wash their faces, turn their jackets back and disappear into the crowd. No one really knows, as it simply wasn't written down, but it would seem reasonable that the locals would start referring to these people as Moorish as they had blackened faces. Whether or not the dancers played up to this will never be known, but again, entertainers are quite happy to add a little mysticism, and the idea of foreign lands to people who would never have travelled much more than five miles from their birthplace is an easy one.

So the name of the tradition of border Morris dancing was born, not the tradition itself. In this day and age, planet woke seems to lump them in with the black and white minstrel show where performers would black up to look like black people only because black people weren't allowed to perform on "white peoples' stages" and the entertainers wanted to bring the vibrant sounds of the black community to white audiences - or at least their version of it. There is a world of difference here.

There are still people out there who think that Morris dancing originated in North Africa, the original home of the Moors. I don't believe there is any North African traditional dancing that looks anything like ours or any historical records referring to Moorish dancing traditions. I am told they have found other cultures as far afield as South America where they use feathers, bells and their version of tatter jackets. I do not think this means that we have taken our tradition from others. I just think this means we are more closely connected than people are willing to believe. I would suggest that any culture that has dancing as part of its expression, would use decoration as part of the performance, and things hanging from your clothing that flare out when you dance would also be used. If you believe that our traditional dances were nicked from other cultures, you would have to believe that we had no dancing tradition on this fair island prior to the

239

fifteenth century. The only people who don't have dancing traditions that go back beyond the stone age are those that live in tundra regions and people whose religious dogma has battered it out of them.

So Morris dancers with blacked-up faces are, in my opinion, following a tradition that was born of the reformation, not some weird quirk of fate that would have necessitated Moorish people being a prominent feature in Herefordshire. Because they would have to have been prominent to affect an entire dancing tradition.

I have heard of people questioning all of this and stating that they believe that the tradition is racist and should be stopped. The Morris Dancing Federation has decided to follow this line of thought. This is because the federation is made up of people who believe that there is only one type of Morris dancing – the Cotswold style, (who do not use face paint). They are happy to see our traditional style lost to time in order to avoid facing a political decision that some may disagree with. As a group of people whose sole task is to preserve one historical aspect of our lives – traditional folk dancing – I think they have failed in their task and should, to a man, stand down and allow honest people to lead the organisation. As far as the people who still believe this narrative and are still offended, despite being given the advantage of a coherent explanation?

Well, they can continue to be offended if that is what they so desperately want. Just don't expect the narrative to change because of their own intransigence.

Misogyny

I don't suggest for one moment that arguing against misogyny is wokism per se, but it does overlap. I have worked in an industry that, although still to this day is male-centric, has welcomed women into the fold and, in the last thirty or so years, has removed the glass ceiling to allow everyone, regardless of gender, race or sexual preference, the opportunity to advance. In my time, I worked with women as peers, I have supervised women, and I have been led by women. Some were good at what they did, some not so good and most were perfectly fine. I even had one woman who was not great at what she did until she got a promotion, then she found her feet and became very good at what she did. In the same period, I also worked with men, some of whom were good, some bad and some gloriously indifferent. The fact is, the split between good, bad and indifferent women was, and probably still is, exactly the same as men. As the Americans are wont to say, Go figure!

There is one constant in the universe – time. Some experts will tell you that not all time is constant, but the fact that time exists everywhere in the universe is. Everything ages, everything dies, everything renews. On the planet Earth, there are two basic life forms, plant and animal. To ensure survival, all those life forms age and die out, but not before creating new life to carry the baton forward. In humans, this involves sex. Sex between opposite sexes. Set aside IVF and Frankenstein-type scientists; this is the only way we keep going. Because of this, it is vital that the two sexes interact sexually. So every time a man approaches a lone woman in a bar and tries to chat her up, that is not sexual harassment; that is just life. If the woman tells the bloke to sling his hook, and he comes back for more, then we might start to look at that scenario. I personally would suggest that a guy should at least give it one extra go. It is, after all, perseverance that has got us to where we are now. If every time a man hears the word no, he slithers off into the corner to tend to his wounded pride; the world would be rather uninhabited. I have no problem with this concept. I have a real problem with people who don't take no for an answer and keep coming back despite the clear signals. I am quite prepared to have them answer for their sins. I am happy to say that I have been instrumental in seeing that this has happened on many occasions.

All this is not really where our issues lay. This game has been played out since the year dot and will carry on for some time to come. The problem is in the way we perceive women in this area. If a woman believes that the best form of contraceptive is a headache pill... held tight between the knees of straightened legs, She is thought by some as being frigid. If a woman enjoys sex and doesn't feel the need to be in any permanent relationship, then she is a floozy, loose woman, trollop and all the other derogative words that we hear. If a man chooses not to engage freely in sex, he is considered thoughtful, decent, maybe a little inadequate, but safe in any event. If he is out on the pull every night – different port, different woman – then he is one of the lads, a good guy, a Jack-the-lad. This narrative needs to be adjusted.

Women in the workplace? Why on earth not? In this country, in the last 470 years, queens have led us for 232 years. As near as makes no difference, half the elapsed time. If that does not seem remarkable, then consider that there were just four of them while there were nine Kings. We have had three female Prime Ministers, and the police and fire brigade have been led by women. I will go out on a limb and say that Cressida Dick, the commissioner of the Met Police up to 2022, was probably the best Commissioner they have had in at least 30 years. Not because of her gender, just the way she went about her business. The fact that she was effectively fired by an incompetent Mayor – who only ever thought about himself – because she would not comply with highly questionable political machinations is probably something that strengthens this point of view.

Despite many an organisation's assertion that they are gender neutral, I believe that they are not. The fact is that men and women tend to look at problems from a different perspective. What we need to establish is that these differences are neither good nor bad, just different. We are not going to resolve this issue by trying to ignore the fact that there are two sexes. We just need to understand that both have equal relevance in the workplace. What we don't want to do, is to stifle the sexual interactions between men and women due to workplace issues overtaking common sense while at the same time ensuring that people don't feel threatened by sexual advances. Essentially keep sexual advances out of the office. You don't have to look too far back to see a time when husbands and wives were not allowed to work in the same office. People were not allowed to have any kind of relationships with fellow workers and if they did, it was a closely guarded secret. Nowadays the gloves are off and such restrictions are considered a breach of human rights. Of course, sexual assault allegations have gone up and there can be tensions around an office when there are relationship problems but that is the price of progress.

Let us look slightly deeper into the role of women in the workplace. The 'rank' of King is higher than that of Queen. This is why QE II's husband was a Duke, not a King because he could not outrank the Monarch. This means that at the highest level, the dominance of men over women is accepted without question, while the dominance of women is almost always questioned. They tried to marry off Queen Elizabeth I. Not because they thought it would make her life more meaningful. No, they wanted the country run by a king, not some flaky, weak-willed woman. History does not tend to support this standpoint.

Language

This whole issue is, of course, a lot deeper than workplace issues. The workplace is where it seems to manifest itself, but we need to look beyond this. We need to change our language before we can make proper inroads. Let's have a look at Language. See if people can see where the root of the problem is.

The word cow is used as a derogatory to describe women who aren't friendly or who are non-compliant, 'Stupid cow won't do as she is told.'

The word bull or bullish is used to describe confidence and prowess – and sometimes stubbornness – in men.

A mare is an unpleasant woman. A nightmare is a bad dream and is often used to describe the worst of situations "a nightmare scenario"

A stallion is used to describe men at the height of their powers.

A vixen is an unpleasant woman

Someone who is foxy is sly and cunning, but often in a positive way.

We use the word witch as a derogative when describing women we don't like. 'Don't bother trying to get to know her; she a witch.'

We use the word wizard to describe men who are very good at what they do. 'Have you seen him playing snooker? He's brilliant, a real wizard.'

Then, of course there is the word "bitch". It is just a word for a female dog but has become so abused that people don't even want to refer to their pet as a bitch. The word dog can be used in so many ways. It can be a derogative when assigned to human behaviour. Why I do not know, but it is milder than the female version. Dog is also used to describe determination. 'he was dogged in his pursuit of the truth'. To dog is to follow someone or something. To be dog-tired is simply strengthening the word tired.

All these and more get into the minds of young people and stay there. These young people grow up having these thoughts seeping into their subconsciousness without knowing it. Look at the cruder end of the language issue. We all hear people being described as a 'prick' or a 'dick' or a 'knob' or the dozens of other synonyms for the male genitals. These are generally thought to be relatively mild rebukes. The use of the female form all of a sudden changes things. Most will believe that 'dropping the C-bomb' is the worst of insults and unutterable. I certainly do not use it.

Why? Why is it that the one part of the female anatomy that gives men and women physical pleasure and is the source of new life is also being used in such a derogatory way? I think that when I scratch the surface of this, I find religion is primarily to blame. Most religious organisations, it seems, have, in the past, used their patriarchal beliefs to subjugate and control women. One only has to look at the catholic church and its offspring, the protestant and orthodox branches, to see this in all its glory. We know of the four gospels of Matthew, Mark, Luke and John, but what of the other ones that the church destroyed or hid away as it didn't fit with their teachings? Was it because

Mary Magdalene or any of the other women held a higher profile than the church approved of? Why is Mary portrayed as a virgin when she clearly was not? Is it because she was unmarried at time of conception, and we can't have the son of god being born a bastard, could we? And the mother could hardly be thought of as a wanton hussy who lay with men outside of wedlock, that's man's job. Why is Mary Magdalene portrayed as a prostitute but no evidence of this is offered or even suggested? Jesus Christ is portrayed as unmarried. Perfectly acceptable in the world in which we live, but two thousand years ago a 35-year-old Jewish man would have been expected to be married and the father of several offspring. If he was not, then I would be surprised if he would have been treated with anything like the respect he apparently received. I think perhaps it is because the patriarchy did not want women to be seen as influential. The Catholic church had always been against anyone other than the church acolytes being able to read. They grudgingly allowed the aristocracy and certain professions, such as medical and law, to read, but they didn't like it. The only reading was the bible, and it was for the church to interpret as they saw fit. They didn't want any old scrubber to come and start arguing the finer points of Christ's teachings. All religious writings were in Latin, just in case someone had the temerity to learn to read. And as for women reading, what was the point? They are just there to produce more Catholics.

Then came along the Protestants. As previously stated, they wanted everyone to read. Men, women, children, rich, poor, whatever. They needed to read so that they could read the English bible as interpreted from Latin by them on behalf of James 1 of England. They did not see that there was any interpreting to do other than that. If it is written down, then that's what happened. So everyone should read this, but only this. They had to eat, sleep and dream it word for word. As for sex, the female form should be avoided at all costs, save for the odd occasion soon after marriage when a family needed to be started to increase the protestant population. Once the family is established, all that should stop in order to concentrate on reading and listening to religious brainwashing. It seemed that any breach of this would be because wanton women were leading good pious men astray. This would seem to indicate that the religious leaders of the time thought that men were weak-minded and women could bend them to their will.

I don't want to believe that the women of biblical times were treated as badly as they have been since the rise of the churches of Christianity, Islam and Judaism, although I am told that in the story of the feeding of the five

249

thousand, that figure referred only to the men. However, this could be a matter of misinterpretation once again. I'm pretty sure the whole story is a misinterpretation.

In the religious turmoil that stemmed from the advance of Protestantism when witch-hunting started to become a thing under the aforementioned King James 1, where did all that come from? I do not believe for a moment that these supposedly intelligent men thought that women were going around casting spells on men to alter their minds and lead them from the path of the true teachings of god. I think it was because some intelligent women felt they had a voice and chose to disagree with the people who had set themselves up as a conduit to their god. They could therefore not be argued against because in so doing, you be arguing with god himself. (I use the masculine deliberately). The women who were putting forward strong ideas that the religious leaders were finding challenging to argue were targeted. Rather than trying to argue with them, they just destroyed their credibility and threw biblical teachings at them to press home their point. They then just burned them in Scotland and drowned or jailed them in England. We also have to remember that the religious teachings were only interpretations by the male hierarchy of the church. These writings were translated from Aramaic and ancient Greek into Latin and then into all sorts of other languages. Many of these writings have been misinterpreted or at least brought into question.

This negative view of women has come from deep in our history and is not going to be easy to shift. We go back to Language because, surely, that is where we need to start. The language of the sexualisation of people needs attention. Despite our woke community wanting to believe that there are more than two sexes, there aren't. As previously posited, you can identify as whatever you want, but whatever that may be, if you have a womb, you are scientifically a woman. Chromosomes don't lie.

There is an ongoing issue with women being paid less for doing the same job. We should be a little careful with this one. If there is a competition for an appointment between a man and a woman who have similar experience, qualifications, and all the rest of it, then there should be parity. But what if, for example, we are talking about the entertainment industry? I am told that when Sandi Toxfig took over on the TV show QI, she was offered less than Stephen Fry had earned for doing the same job. She argued this. I think this should have been easy to argue against. It is the entertainment industry; you are not being paid for doing a job; you are being paid because you attract an audience. If you attract a similar audience based on your ability and following, then yes. But I think Mr Fry has a huge following, and Ms Toxfig would struggle to emulate that, as brilliant as she is. I play the guitar. I could not go to the BBC and demand the same fee as Eric Clapton for making an appearance. It matters not how good or bad I am; I don't have the same draw as Mr Clapton, so he gets the money, and I don't. If industry could prove that the reason for the pay disparity was the fact that the man was bringing in more custom, I think they would have a point, and I think that the woke brigade should know this. It would, of course, have to work both ways. If a lesser-known man took over from Ms Toxfig, then there is no reason for him to earn the same as her if it can be shown that he had a smaller following. My personal problem in this area is that women appear to be dumped when the powers-that-be believe that they are not pretty enough for the telly. No one ever told Trevor MacDonald or Bruce Forsythe that they were too old and ugly.

There are other disparities that have been poorly handled. In the Wimbledon tennis tournament, Women are paid the same as men despite the fact that the men have to play the best of five sets and the women only the best of three. If the pay is the same, then the work rate or, in this case, the set count should be. Otherwise it is not equality - unless you can show that the women are attracting a larger audience. Perhaps the way around it is to ensure they get paid the same for each set (or potential set) so that everyone gets paid a set amount per set but will receive payment for three sets in the case of women and five in the case of men. This would mean that either the men get two-fifths more than the women or the women play five-set matches.

When we consider sports, it is right that where strength, speed or size is a deciding factor, then the sport should have men's sides and women's sides. But what of other sports like darts, snooker and such like? Why split them? What possible advantage or disadvantage does one gender have over another in these endeavours? Mix them up. If women want to have their own tournament, then they can't complain if the men have one of their own, but the controlling organisations can say that they would only recognise mixed sport in official tournaments where gender has no influencing factor.

The issue of transgender people in sports has been hotly debated. I think it is a fairly simple argument. If their musculature or their bulk is not affected by the change, then it is hardly fair that a person with a masculine musculature should compete against women in sports where bulk, strength and speed are a factor. I recall the South African 'female' 800-metre runner who was smashing international records left, right and centre. This

253

athlete looked like a man and ran like a man, so the question was, 'Is this person a man?' There was a lot of prevarication and a lot of people saying that it was not straight forward as one might think. Well, it is. We can determine medically, with accuracy, what gender a person is. If this person is a man, then what they are doing is cheating – pure and simple. It does not matter that they have 'reassigned' their gender. The issue is, does the body operate as a male or a female? If this person wanted to be in a female team, then choose something that does not rely on speed, strength or bulk.

The issue with women-only teams in any walk of life has all sorts of problems that people seem to be unwilling to address. If we want the best people in any job, sport, or any other activity, then find the best people. In the job market, there are very few instances where sex, sexuality or race have any kind of real place – you wouldn't put a 6'7" Afro-Caribbean male basketball player undercover to discover the nefarious goings-on in the Long Melford, Women's' Institute, for example. I think one would probably need a middle-aged, middle England white East Anglian female for that. Nor would you insert a female soprano into a male voice choir, I think we are on safe ground there. Having said all that, there are plenty of companies that only, or at best predominantly, employ women and plenty who only employ from their own ethnic minority group for no other reason than they don't want to employ people who fall outside those parameters. How can you possibly hope to find the best person for the job if you preclude the majority of the workforce. I think this prejudicial treatment is counterproductive at best, but if that is what you want, then those that support it cannot complain when a company only wants to employ men. Sexism, racism, and any other ~ism you care to mention is a two-way street. Let's face it; we are better off without it altogether.

The strange world of Morris dancing has debated the subject of female dancers for years. As previously mentioned, there are nine different styles of Morris dancing, the most prominent of which is the Cotswold tradition. These are the ones that dress predominantly in white and use hankies and small sticks and bells on their shins. Many of the 'sides' (the word used to describe a Morris dancing team) in this particular tradition are strictly men only. Some would not even communicate with women from other sides purely because they were women, and 'women shouldn't be Morris dancing'. Imagine! Women wanting to dance? Whatever next! Many have recently relented and allowed women in. Some have started a women's side to dance at the same events as them, but not together.

There are some who have started women-only sides. Now this is perfectly fine, but what it means is that they can no longer complain about men-only sides. What's good for the goose... It seems to me that the current state of affairs is quite nice: some men-only, some women-only, but mainly mixed. The side with which I am involved is a 'Border Morris' side. This is the tradition that originated from the Welsh English borders and practice fighting dances. Probably more reason to have a men-only side, but I know of no border Morris side that is men-only as a policy. Ours certainly is not – although we have trouble finding female musicians, but this is not for want of trying.

Culture

In some cultures, adultery is seen as the woman's fault in all circumstances. Some of those cultures believe that if a woman was raped, it was probably her fault. Other cultures seem to believe that women simply can't be raped. I am reminded of a story many years ago in Africa, when a white judge questioned the evidence of a rape victim. He apparently held a sewing needle with a large eye and asked the woman to thread it with cotton while he held it. Naturally, when she tried, he just moved the needle out of the way. This was his justification of his belief that women could avoid the attentions of a man if they so desired. Fortunately, dinosaurs like that are now

256

where they belong – in their graves. But there is still a belief in some cultures that if they don't want it, they can avoid it unless it is with her husband, then she has to comply! If you believe that, then you should take a long look at yourself.

Rape trials are fraught with dangers because all it takes is three members of a jury out of twelve to be of this mindset, and it wouldn't matter if you had all the evidence in the world; at the very best, you would end up with no decision and a whole new trial to endure. I was witness to a trial of a 40-year-old man who was seen having full sexual intercourse with a nine-year-old girl, by the mother of the girl. Forensic science confirmed the evidence provided, and there could have been no doubt that vaginal penetration had taken place. In this country, there are no defences to this. Anyone over twenty-one is deemed to have sufficient control over anyone under twelve – the age before which one is not allowed to consent to sex – to be able to avoid a sexual encounter (actually the legal age in the UK is 16, but there is a grey area between 12 and 16 where they 'can' consent but the older, more responsible person should not seek it or accept the consent or succumb to the attentions of the minor. No such grey area below that age). Yet, in this case, the jury could not come to a decision. This can only mean that at least three of the members thought that it was perfectly fine for a forty-year-old man to have sex with a nine-year-old or that it was entirely the nine-year-old's fault. If either scenario is true, then I would suggest that the decision those jurors came to be a result of cultural beliefs and practices and not, as it should have been, a review of the evidence in light of the laws of this country. Fortunately, there was a re-trial with a different jury, and he was convicted.

In conclusion, to say, "I like women; my mother was one," is a little too flippant and entirely inaccurate (not the bit about my mother, she is definitely a woman). But to say that I will base my opinion on someone based only on their gender is ludicrous. In so doing, you are casting one opinion on over half the world's population. There are awful women out there, and there are incredible women out there, and every other woman falls somewhere inside those two extremes – just like men. The only time when gender matters is when you are looking for a sexual relationship – or for someone to go undercover in the Long Melford Women's Institute – everything else is bluster.

Cultural Appropriation

Cultural appropriation. A phrase that I believe should be expunged from the dictionary forever. This is a derogatory phrase that appears to be aimed primarily at white people who take on the dress code, music, hairstyles and/or lifestyles of a different culture because they like what that culture stands for. Where is the problem with that? We don't complain about people coming to England and becoming 'Westernised'. We just think of them as integrating, so why can't it work the other way? Who are they harming? There are many and varied criticisms that can be placed at the door of Axel Rose, lead singer for Guns 'n' Roses, for example but cultural appropriation because he chooses to wear his hair in dreadlocks? That is just plain laziness from the finger-pointers. Personally, I think it is cultural snobbery from those of the culture being 'appropriated' who are doing the complaining. They are the ones at fault here, not those who choose to live their lives how they want to without causing harm to anyone else.

On the subject of cancel culture, I need to say something about those who want to expunge from history those who they believe to have been wrong in what they did way back in history when different attitudes, different priorities and different belief structures prevailed. I find it astonishing that the middle eastern religions committed unspeakable acts of barbarism, murder, rape and cruelty in the name of their god and, not only do people accept this, but actually support it. When you speak about 17th and 18th century colonisers, some of whom were cruel and barbarous but most were just people who thought they were doing the world a favour – whether you believe they were or not – are being expunged from history even if they did truly wonderful and generous things outside of the colonisation sphere. I cannot stress more firmly that this is wrong. It is counterproductive, and it doesn't help. What they are trying to do is rewrite history. That path does not lead anywhere good. We all learn not just from our own mistakes but from everyone else's as well. I am reminded of the campaign to rid Oxford University of the statue of Cecil John Rhodes because he was a colonialist. One of the most vociferous of the campaigners was, in fact, a Rhodes Scholar and so would not have had the opportunity to voice his views without the scheme that was put in place by the very person he was trying to delete from history. Forget about the fact that the entire population of the known world has been invading and colonising for as long as humans have been a societal species. We only have to look at it from the fifteen hundreds to know that the whole of Europe was doing the same. Whether we like it or not, CJ Rhodes was a cog in a much bigger machine, so to cancel him, one would have to cancel a whole swathe of Dutch, French, Spanish, and Russian colonialists. Don't even start on the idea that the Muslim peoples of the Arabian Peninsula had colonised the whole of the Sahara. It may not sit well with modern thinking, but their actions have shaped the modern world.

Africa and the Americas would be entirely different beasts were it not for them. No one knows if this has been for the better or not. The fact is that it happened, and we have to deal with it. Taking down statues and trying to wipe people from history will create confusion and will not allow people to take lessons from these actions.

I am aware that history is written by the victors and, as such, much of what we learn may well not be that accurate. But trying to change it for something that is equally inaccurate cannot be an improvement, even if the dialogue makes for easier reading. I was watching a program on TV where a well-known celeb was going to countries that one would not normally think of as a place to visit. All he was doing was putting a positive spin on countries that get a bad press. That is fine, but it all went a little bit south when he went to Zimbabwe. Because I lived in that part of the world for fifteen years, I have a little knowledge of the history.

Bearing in mind my previous comment about how history is written, I have to draw from what I was taught and combine it with other known facts to try to find the centre of the Ven diagram. What I was taught was that Rhodes had been successfully prospecting in South Africa and decided that he wanted the British Empire to have a clear route from Cape Town to Cairo that was owned by the

British. There had been discussions in Europe about how they should enter the areas of this new world and how they should conduct themselves. An agreement was signed to say that negotiation should be at the heart of it and not violent, invasive forces (It seems to me that the violence came after they were established, and the locals decided that they didn't want them anymore). To this end, Rhodes crossed the Limpopo River into what is now Zimbabwe. For some years prior to this, a man called Mzilikazi had a falling out with King Chaka, the leader of the Zulus. Mzilikazi took his supporters – all male – and left to cross the same river. There they invaded the local tribes, killed the men and took the women to start their own tribe. Before long, He was top-johnny-banana for the whole area, and anyone coming or going through his territory had to either go through him or meet the business end of their assegais.

Rhodes was aware of this and sought an audience. This was granted after about six months of prevarication and a negotiation was started. Essentially, what Rhodes was saying, was that he wanted to dig holes and collect Gold and diamonds. Both these materials were useless to the locals. Gold was too soft and too heavy to make anything useful with, and Diamonds were too hard and, at the end of the day, they were just stones. So he wanted to come into the area, dig their holes, farm and hunt so that they could feed themselves and maybe use the locals for labour for remuneration – he wasn't a slaver. This was eventually agreed upon, and Rhodes had his foothold. The area that he negotiated was ill-defined because it had no borders, and Mzilikazi was himself relatively new to the area. So Rhodes made his own mind up as to what the area was. Part of the landscape in the area where Mzilikazi's new tribe, the Ndebele, had settled held a ruined town. This is now referred to as Great Zimbabwe. It is unique in the area as it is the only ruined city in the whole of Sub-Saharan Africa that was built before Europeans came. No one truly knows who built it. It certainly predated the Ndebele people, and African people weren't builders as they were semi-nomadic, moving around to follow the seasonal food sources. The best guess is that people from the Sahara managed to get there. It had previously been thought that the people of the desert regions couldn't handle the pestilence of the wetter areas of the Congo and the savanna, so they had given up trying to colonise that part of Africa. Compelling DNA evidence has now suggested that some got through. These people were builders and so would have had the wherewithal to build a town wherever they settled. No one knows how it was ruined and what happened to the residents. Whatever the story, it was clear that the African people treated the city with suspicion and avoided the place. Of course, when the

263

British. There had been discussions in Europe about how they should enter the areas of this new world and how they should conduct themselves. An agreement was signed to say that negotiation should be at the heart of it and not violent, invasive forces (It seems to me that the violence came after they were established, and the locals decided that they didn't want them anymore). To this end, Rhodes crossed the Limpopo River into what is now Zimbabwe. For some years prior to this, a man called Mzilikazi had a falling out with King Chaka, the leader of the Zulus. Mzilikazi took his supporters – all male – and left to cross the same river. There they invaded the local tribes, killed the men and took the women to start their own tribe. Before long, He was top-johnny-banana for the whole area, and anyone coming or going through his territory had to either go through him or meet the business end of their assegais.

Rhodes was aware of this and sought an audience. This was granted after about six months of prevarication and a negotiation was started. Essentially, what Rhodes was saying, was that he wanted to dig holes and collect Gold and diamonds. Both these materials were useless to the locals. Gold was too soft and too heavy to make anything useful with, and Diamonds were too hard and, at the end of the day, they were just stones. So he wanted to come into the area, dig their holes, farm and hunt so that they could feed themselves and maybe use the locals for labour for remuneration – he wasn't a slaver. This was eventually agreed upon, and Rhodes had his foothold. The area that he negotiated was ill-defined because it had no borders, and Mzilikazi was himself relatively new to the area. So Rhodes made his own mind up as to what the area was. Part of the landscape in the area where Mzilikazi's new tribe, the Ndebele, had settled held a ruined town. This is now referred to as Great Zimbabwe. It is unique in the area as it is the only ruined city in the whole of Sub-Saharan Africa that was built before Europeans came. No one truly knows who built it. It certainly predated the Ndebele people, and African people weren't builders as they were semi-nomadic, moving around to follow the seasonal food sources. The best guess is that people from the Sahara managed to get there. It had previously been thought that the people of the desert regions couldn't handle the pestilence of the wetter areas of the Congo and the savanna, so they had given up trying to colonise that part of Africa. Compelling DNA evidence has now suggested that some got through. These people were builders and so would have had the wherewithal to build a town wherever they settled. No one knows how it was ruined and what happened to the residents. Whatever the story, it was clear that the African people treated the city with suspicion and avoided the place. Of course, when the

Europeans got there, they just raided the place and stole the unique relics, but it was already a ruined city by then.

Rhodes went further North and settled close to where Harare is based. He called the new town that he created Salisbury. Mzilikazi eventually died and was succeeded by a chap called Lobengula. This was a savvy chap. He didn't know what these pale-faced people wanted with diamonds; he just knew that they prized them, so he collected them. He mainly got his men to 'steal' them from mines that they worked on. Legend has it that Lobengula thought Rhodes had found out what was happening and that he had all these stones. He believed that Rhodes was hunting him down to get them back, so he went on the run.

Meanwhile, Rhodes, who was blissfully unaware of the treasures held by Lobengula, was looking to negotiate new areas to dig and sent two Americans, who were part of his retinue, to find him. They did find him, and, thinking that he was doomed, Lobengula immediately handed over all the diamonds. The Americans were also blissfully unaware of these diamonds and knew that Rhodes knew nothing of them as well. So they both looked at each other, looked at Lobengula, looked at the diamond and said, "Thank you very much", and disappeared, never to be heard from again. I don't think anyone knows what happened to

264

Lobengula, but he was the last recognised tribal leader of the Ndebele. They remained in the southern part of what is now Zimbabwe and were almost wiped out by the ever-delightful Mugabi.

In the TV show that I was watching, the person who was the 'guide' assigned to lead our celeb around took him to the ruins and told him that it was built by the people of Zimbabwe and was occupied for hundreds of years where they lived a peaceful and idyllic life – children gambolling in the meadows, housewifes singing sweet tunes to the babies as they hung their washing out, men tilling the land – until Rhodes came bursting in, all guns blazing and ripped the place apart while enslaving the population. She didn't seem to want to explain why this was the only known pre-European city anywhere in sub-Saharan Africa and why it would be that one single tribe suddenly started building things that would never have been seen anywhere prior to that time. Also, no explanation as to why they decided to stop there and build nothing else or even rebuild the ruins after it was destroyed. It was also the only occasion where Rhodes initiated any violence towards any population anywhere in Africa. Why would he suddenly change tack for no reason? He wasn't being impeded, so why antagonise his only source of labour? While I can't say which version is true – or at least more accurate than the other – it does seem to me that

Zimbabwe has rewritten the story based on no evidence whatsoever, and it is too full of holes. I couldn't say what Rhodes was like or whether he used his labour as slaves and subjugated them, but there is no written record of anything like that from anyone. We have to remember that, not only were the indigenous population not builders, but they also had no written language either, so all their history was word of mouth with some rock paintings thrown in. I believe Rhodes kept meticulous records. I am sure that rewriting history to suit their sensibilities may well make them feel better, but I can't see how it helps anyone. Sub-Saharan African history pre-Vasco Da Gama is virtually all word-of-mouth and almost non-existent. Any written language would have been confined to the east coast, where trading routes between Arabia, Africa and India have been going on for thousands of years. Why make it different? They say that necessity is the mother of invention. I truly believe this. These people had no reason to build cities being semi-nomadic. The necessity was not there. Because there were no cities, the need for complex communication was not there, so the written word was not needed. They lived, they hunted, and they cultivated to support their small communities. They then moved on to where the water and food supplies were more plentiful when they needed to. Cancelling colonialists isn't going to change that.

266

Shariya Law

Lets go out with a bang in this chapter. It may come as no surprise that, given this is a monologue about pub conversations, I haven't had the opportunity to have a full-blown chat about this with a Muslim person in a pub. Not really their scene. I have, however seen and heard plenty on radio, news media and television to know that I don't believe there is any benefit in this idea that Shariya law should be introduced for the benefit of the Muslim population whatsoever. It is divisive and pointless. We will brush over the fact that when I go abroad, whether I believe the laws of the host country are good or not, I expect to be held to account for any breach of them. I therefore expect anyone in this country, whether as a resident or visitor, to be held to our standards whatever they think of them.

I think the nub of the issue is a little more involved but a fairly simple concept nonetheless. The vast majority of Shariya law reflects our laws. Things that insist that people don't nick other people's stuff or assault them or con them out of their life's savings. If they do reflect our laws, why have another law that overrides it. For all the other parts that do not reflect our laws, they don't because we think them either unnecessary or in contravention of our laws.

This goes equally for the statutes and the punishment for the breaches. So there is no point in having them.

My bigger concern is the issue of division. What the Muslim supporters of the Shariya law argument are suggesting is that they want to be treated as being separate from the rest of society. That they believe their way is better than everyone else's. They get in a big huff when people go into a country that is controlled under Shariya and breach their laws. They believe that people should comply regardless of their own belief system. I cannot transfer my legal system to their country under any circumstance. If that is the case, why would anyone think it ok to do so here. I believe that we should all be treated equally under the law. We should all be judged by the same standards and if anyone thinks that they don't want to abide by our laws, they can go to a country who has laws that they agree with. This is not to say one should not question the law. They just have to comply with it until it is changed. And that goes equally throughout society whether you can trace your ancestry back to the year dot on this muddy Island or are first generation.

If anyone thinks that this statement is in somewhat prejudiced, then I say that it is the polar opposite of prejudice. If the etymology of the word is 'before being proven evidentially', I am saying that everyone should be

268

judged after evidence is provided under the laws of this land.

Multi-culturalism

What in the name of all that is holy is that. We are all the same. We all have the same wants and needs. We all want to be happy, healthy and safe. The idea that some people want their women to hide behind swathes of clothing because some bloke who lived fifteen hundred years ago said that his god said they must, does not change that. Nor the fact that some people don't eat certain foods or display their beliefs in different ways change anything. All it does is identify people who believe they are different, but how different are they? You'd never be able to tell from skeletal remains what culture you followed. There is a line in a song that I like in which the writer is being witheringly sarcastic about rich folk's opinions and wonders why poor folk put them on pedestals. The line is, 'coffin dust is a fate for everyone.' Now I know that we all aren't necessarily going to be interred in a coffin, but the sentiment is bang-on. We all end up the same way – deceased. That includes all the different faiths, races, creeds and whatever other divisions you choose to insert into our lives. As far as where we go after we die, I'll let you know for sure when I get there, but I reckon I could guess fairly accurately.

England is one of the most cosmopolitan countries. It is an Island and we have been receiving visitors – some welcome, some not ever so – from the very beginning. Despite this, there is separation. We only have to look at London: Brixton has always been considered an Afro/Caribbean stronghold. Golders green is associated with the Jewish community, Hounslow with the Asian community and in north London one will find a strong Greek Cypriot community. Of course central London is the stronghold of Russian oligarchs by all accounts. There are many more groups and sub-groups. No one has forced these people to live in these communities, there are no laws preventing people from living where they choose. I can see how people would find succour in amongst familiar languages and customs, but it saddens me somewhat that some people feel they need to do this. There is probably an element of people looking for somewhere to live who happens to know someone who knows someone who has a flat to rent. I can see that this would be within their community, so I am not pointing accusing fingers, I just feel that integration is better.

I read a newspaper headline recently that stated the pro-Palestinian marches in London were proof that multi-culturalism doesn't work. Now given the comment at the beginning of the first paragraph on this subject, I should find this difficult to argue. But I'll have a go. No, it does not. It may show that the lack of cultural cohesion in Israel/Palestine/Gaza is not working. It may even show that some members of that protest were deeply intolerant of people who they see as being outside their cultural parameters. When people start shouting things that encourage jihad, then it simply shows that those that are doing this are in favour of violence to put their point across. What it does not say is that we should all be divided up and separated. What it does not say is that we can't all live together. Nor does it say that the members of the demo necessarily agree with the chants. There is strong evidence to suggest that these chants are coming from what we used to refer to as 'rent-a-mob'. They are inserted into these demos to destroy the credibility of the marchers. Hamas is a terrorist organisation. It goes about its business by threatening, kidnapping and killing people who have little means to defend themselves in order to try to make immoveable politicians move. This is unacceptable, if they want to have a go at someone, have a go at the politicians that are repressing their people. Israel, on the other hand is repressing the people who they displaced after the second world war. They treat the Palestinians as an inconvenience they could do without all because the Palestinians want to follow their own religious dogma instead of the Jewish one. Come on guys, they have been displaced from their home. You may feel that you have a god-given right to that land, but so do they. Have a little sympathy and play nicely. They still need somewhere to live comfortably. There isn't a member of a terrorist organisation in the world who wakes up in the morning saying that life is wonderful and they are living the dream. If you want to stop terrorism, take away the causal factors, easy, eh?

I would also add that demonstrating in London is not going to achieve anything. We hear that it is there to highlight the issues. Anyone who are not aware of the issues in the Middle East have been living with their heads in a part of their bodies where the sun never shines. No politician in Israel is going to see these demonstrations and say to themselves, 'Oh, I never thought of it that way, everything we believed in over the last five thousand years is all wrong. I'll change my policies immediately.' If anyone in London believe that the demonstrators make a good point, they will be able to do nothing with that information. Our politicians will do whatever they will do that is exigent to their own personal development with or without the demo. All the demonstration achieves is to clog up the streets of London and annoy the locals whether or not they support the cause and allow the rent-a-mob to disrupt. I get freedom of speech and all that, but

I don't think that this is the way forward. It's just another of those things that create divisions where none should exist.

So the message to one and all is, welcome to our humble abode. Live, love and be happy. Please treat everyone on this little patch of mud we call Great Britain with respect and we will try to reciprocate. Don't complain if you don't.

Solution?

How about this to get the blood flowing. To sort out all these issues, the entire world must get together and build a huge impregnable compound. No one can get in, no one can get out once the doors are locked. Then gather every high-ranking politician throughout the world and put them all in there. Add to the mix every mega rich person – the ones that control the politicians – and freeze all their assets. Give them everything their hearts desire: food, weapons luxuries, poisons, everything and anything except for access to any wealth. They will have some sort of bag over their heads or a way that will prevent them from identifying anyone in the compound and the removal of all identifying features so they can't recognise or prejudge anyone and no names are to be used. Remove all existing laws so that they have no restrictions whatsoever then leave them there for a month, two months, however long we think they need to see how they fair in this no-holds-barred free-for-all . Tell them that they will not be allowed out until all the solutions have been found and that their assets will remain frozen until everything has been sorted out properly and put into place. After an appropriate amount of time, check in and see how it has gone. One of two things would have happened, in my view. They would all have started communicating and come up with solutions or they will have destroyed themselves. If they have worked together, then the world would be a better place. If the latter scenario is true and only a handful remain, incarcerate the survivors for the rest of their lives so that their poison does not infect anyone.

The advantages are plain. While they are in the compound, the rest of the world can get on with their lives without politicians screwing everything up and the world will be able to live peace. When the experiment is concluded, if they have worked together as they are always saying they do, serious solutions can be put in place to make the world a better place. If no solutions have been found and they have wiped themselves out, the world can only be a better place without them. In any event, it is the people who are causing the problem who will be sorting them out and that has to be right.

THE NOT-SO-BIG C

There are not many inhabitants of this oblate spheroid on which we live – the Earth that is – that have not been affected by the covid 19 virus. The entire world's population have all of a sudden become pharmaceutical eggheads who think they can wax lyrical about the life cycle of a virus. This is a good thing, as I do not have to spend time giving the world the benefit of my woeful lack of knowledge on this subject in these pages. That being said, I have no issue with people passing opinions. It's what I do, so why should other people be disallowed? We are all sentient beings who, while we may not have specific training, do have the capability to read the articles that are being produced on a minute-by-minute basis. The difference is that your opinion is what you are entitled to, but we cannot suppose that we can foist our opinions on others to the point where they have to follow your unenlightened viewpoint. The scientists, on the other hand, have done their time in universities and labs to be able to say with some confidence that their opinion is valid and people should follow their advice. Or at least listen to it and enable themselves to make more informed decisions. But why is it, then, that all these experts are so far away from a consensus? They all had similar training. They all worked in the same sort of labs, and they all wanted the same outcome. Well, let us try to examine this in detail using nothing more than common sense, a basic knowledge of how the body works and an ability to read.

First of all, we have to acknowledge that politicians have got involved in this to a point where they are dictating which parts of the scientists' advice are being made public. Politicians do not care a jot about how the population is actually being affected. They only want to control the message and railroad people into thinking that their way is the only way. As a result of this, it is nigh on impossible to get a proper unabridged account of what has happened over the last covid affected years. Every piece of statistical analysis has been designed to keep everyone on message. It is all accurate in and of itself. It is the context that is being abused by politicians. One has to be aware of the language that prefixes everything that is being said.

Example: The UK government started producing statistics about the progress of COVID quite early on. They were only going a few weeks before they changed how the stats were to be disseminated. This meant that deaths were recorded as 'covid related' if a person died within 28 days of a positive test. Why 28 days? The way that it was reported was significant, and the BBC are past masters at playing with language like this in order to railroad people into thinking the way they want you to think. They would say something to the effect of, 'The number of people who have died with COVID in the last 24 hours – that is, those who have died within 28 days of a positive test – is [add number].' They would then introduce a guest who is there to speak about the latest figures, and so the conversation would start something like, 'So, Mr [science boffin], these are quite damning figures; thousands of people have died of COVID...' So they change the preposition 'with' to 'of' and use this throughout the rest of the article. This happened on an almost daily basis, so it was no mistake. The BBC were manipulating their audience. This may seem pedantic, but is it? To die of covid is fairly unambiguous. To die with COVID says very little but does pose at least three further questions: Firstly, of that number, specifically, how many died of COVID? Secondly, how many died of something else, but the death was exacerbated or at least brought forward by the presence of the virus? Thirdly, how many were run over by a bus and just happened to have had a positive test 27 days earlier?

There are other questions one could also ask, like how many of those who were run over by a bus had had the virus within that time frame but had not tested. We could also argue that the LF tests were not accurate. I have heard several tales of someone having all the classic symptoms but still testing negative, while the person with whom they lived had little or no symptoms but tested positive. The person with the symptom was not allowed to isolate because of their test, and the symptom-free person was forced to. Makes no sense. There are too many questions left unasked to count here, but it does suggest that we were not getting anywhere near the complete picture.

One of the ways I tried to circumvent these attempts by the government to control the conversation was to look at all the statistics and compare them. There was another statistic that was never really referred to, and that was 'those who have covid on their death certificate.' This figure was generally slightly higher than the 28-day one, but I realised before too long that this one also posed a few questions. The fact that one has COVID on the death certificate does not tell anyone who has not had the benefit of viewing the full medical record the actual cause of death. That person could have died of an in-growing toenail and just happened to pick up the virus in the throes of death. We don't know. All I know is that we don't know. Unfortunately, there is a huge portion of our population who would not believe our government if they told us the grass was green but would be prepared to swallow these ridiculous stats because they show the government in a poor light. I would prefer accurate and full figures so I can make my own mind up.

We have all heard many people expounding on the terrible performance of the government in response to this crisis by comparing us with other countries. The problem with this is that every other country's politicians had a completely different agenda, so they would use different criteria to disseminate their information. We also have the very real issue of how many people who were living in very rural areas, even in 'first world' countries, had no access to any kind of testing facilities. How many people in rural Africa were even aware of the virus? South America would have similar issues. There could have been millions more infections than any of us realised. There can have been no real accuracy in the records of the USA. Russia would never give anything approaching an accurate picture. Most African politicians could not give a toss as long as they were a) not infected and b) had a ready supply of decent Scotch. And China?

It is my belief that the UK chose their methods for purely political reasons. If you are going to respond to a crisis, the population needs to believe that they have a real crisis, so there is no problem in making the problem seem worse than it is at first. This is not to say there was no crisis, that is clearly not the case. Nor am I saying the crisis was not deadly, just that I can't trust the government to tell me accurate, unsullied figures. In doing this, they can do their crisis management and adjust their figures to suit at the

280

appropriate time when they need to show that their methods are having a positive effect. So they use the figures to control the population initially, then reassure them towards the end. We all saw how strict the New Zealand government was in response to this crisis, and everyone seemed to think we should do the same. What we did not see is how the population of New Zealand were taking the restrictions. It appeared to me that those who supported the PM thought she did very well, and those who didn't, thought she went too far and brought the economy to its knees. We also did not take into account population mix, population density, ease of access to the country from outside the borders and a plethora of other factors that worked for NZ but could never have worked for the UK. It is quite clear to me that the response in this country was not so different to everywhere else. That is to say, the people who generally supported the government's position thought they did OK. Everyone else thought that we were led to hell in a handbasket by our leaders. With the benefit of the alternative being purely hypothetical and therefore incapable of disproof, I can say with all the certainty I can muster that any other leader would have done things a little differently but would have had the same or very similar actual result. It is what the statistics would have said that would have been different according

281

We have all heard many people expounding on the terrible performance of the government in response to this crisis by comparing us with other countries. The problem with this is that every other country's politicians had a completely different agenda, so they would use different criteria to disseminate their information. We also have the very real issue of how many people who were living in very rural areas, even in 'first world' countries, had no access to any kind of testing facilities. How many people in rural Africa were even aware of the virus? South America would have similar issues. There could have been millions more infections than any of us realised. There can have been no real accuracy in the records of the USA. Russia would never give anything approaching an accurate picture. Most African politicians could not give a toss as long as they were a) not infected and b) had a ready supply of decent Scotch. And China?

It is my belief that the UK chose their methods for purely political reasons. If you are going to respond to a crisis, the population needs to believe that they have a real crisis, so there is no problem in making the problem seem worse than it is at first. This is not to say there was no crisis, that is clearly not the case. Nor am I saying the crisis was not deadly, just that I can't trust the government to tell me accurate, unsullied figures. In doing this, they can do their crisis management and adjust their figures to suit at the appropriate time when they need to show that their methods are having a positive effect. So they use the figures to control the population initially, then reassure them towards the end. We all saw how strict the New Zealand government was in response to this crisis, and everyone seemed to think we should do the same. What we did not see is how the population of New Zealand were taking the restrictions. It appeared to me that those who supported the PM thought she did very well, and those who didn't, thought she went too far and brought the economy to its knees. We also did not take into account population mix, population density, ease of access to the country from outside the borders and a plethora of other factors that worked for NZ but could never have worked for the UK. It is quite clear to me that the response in this country was not so different to everywhere else. That is to say, the people who generally supported the government's position thought they did OK. Everyone else thought that we were led to hell in a handbasket by our leaders. With the benefit of the alternative being purely hypothetical and therefore incapable of disproof, I can say with all the certainty I can muster that any other leader would have done things a little differently but would have had the same or very similar actual result. It is what the statistics would have said that would have been different according

281

to the political agenda of whoever would have been in place.

I remember listening to the news of the spread as it seemed to steadily edge its way westward. Even then, I thought that it was too neat. International air travel meant that infected people would have been all over the world. It is only speculation, so this is not provable, but I think the entire world has been led astray. But there are many myths out there that can be dispensed with. Although there are quiet voices suggesting that it may not have started in China, circumstantial evidence is overwhelming. We have a huge lab that is dealing with virus control in Wuhan. Wuhan is clearly the epicentre, QED.

There were also conspiracy theorists that suggested that the virus was manmade. While I would never put anything past the Chinese political machine, there is evidence to the contrary. The biggest and most challenging to circumnavigate is the idea that manmade viruses do not tend to mutate. This is one of the reasons that the HIV rumours have never gone away; it has never mutated. The way it survives, I believe, is to hide or disguise itself until it is ready to pounce. Viruses have only one aim, survival. It needs a host to survive as they don't have all the necessary equipment to survive on their own. If they kill the host, they either die or have to find another host. So best case scenario for them is that the host survives. The problem is that the hosts don't really welcome them, and the immune systems try to kill them off when they invade your body. The way this virus survives, unlike HIV, is to constantly change to try to avoid or override the body's immune systems. They mutate. This one has clearly continued to mutate throughout the crisis, so probably not manmade. Although there is another theory that Wuhan's scientists used an existing flu-type virus and augmented it with nerve agents. This would damage that supposition. Given that the person telling me this had some medical experience. He was a long covid sufferer and told me that there were 53 symptoms associated with the condition – way above its nearest rival. He believes that when you stripped away the flu symptoms, what you were left with was various forms of nerve damage. I have no way of proving or disproving this and the authorities would never admit to anything like this anyway. But it's worth pondering.

I am fortunate enough to have never suffered from the worst symptoms of this virus. I was in Kenya over the 2019 Christmas period, which meant travelling long distances on aircraft that had a system seemingly designed to propagate infectious microbes and being in a country with a strong migrant Chinese population looking after their mining interests. It came as no surprise then that during

February, the whole household was sick with flu-like symptoms, dry cough and inhibited olfactory senses. It couldn't possibly have been COVID because it only existed in China at that time... didn't it? Because one of the biggest cities in that part of China, which had a population that was in and out of Beijing and so to the rest of the world, would never have allowed that virus to spread beyond its borders. Yeah, right. The idea that COVID had not entered the world population soon after it was released into the Wuhan air just does not sit right. We know that China does not share information with anyone unless it's in their own interest. Why would they start doing that now? Africa is being slowly – by stealth – taken over by China. There is a huge Chinese population in Kenya. Many of them are people that China has decided they don't want as citizens anymore. To me, it is not beyond the realms of possibility that Africa was rife with it while we were there. They just hadn't put a name to it.

PPE

I have all sorts of problems with this sort of stuff. I recall during the first months of the crisis. People were going to supermarkets in their cars. You could see them getting out of their cars, wearing surgical gloves. They would then proceed into the store with a trolley and go around picking things up and putting them down again, then going to the checkout and eventually leaving the shop wearing the same gloves. It was as if they thought that the surface of gloves was not going to transfer germs in the same way as bare skin. No one seemed to think about it for a moment. If they did, it was very much a case of, 'I don't give a toss about anyone else; I'm more than happy to spread it as long as I don't pick up the virus.' The whole point was that the virus could live on a surface for a short period and could be transferred by attaching itself to a person to be deposited further down the line. They would wait for someone to transfer them from a surface onto their hands and from there to that person's insides, where they could then carry on with their business. What they would not do is take a look at the hand being presented and say, 'Hmm, no thank you, i don't do plastic, bad for the environment, I'll wait for an ungloved person.' The wearing of gloves would never do anything to prevent any of that spread. The only way gloves could be effective would be to use them in the same way as surgeons. That is to say, change them every time you move on to a different surface. Dispose of them safely and repeat. The problem is that if you followed that procedure, it would be an environmental disaster. The damage that was caused by using them incorrectly was pretty devastating. Imagine how many of these non-biodegradable things got into the system in the first year, and imagine what it would have been like if they used them correctly.

I am not a big fan of anti-bacs at the best of times. It was these substances that created the super-bug. Soap and water are as effective as it just washes the bugs off the hands and straight down the drain. If an anti-bac kills 99.9% of germs, then the last 0.1% must be immune to the stuff or at least resistant to it. When they start off again, the entire colony will have the same resistance. The more powerful the anti-bac, the more resilient the germs will become. What really got my goat was advertisers saying that their products killed viruses as well. We know this is a lie, but the advertising authority let it slide. If it were that easy, they would never have had to develop a specific anti-viral. I'm sure they were doing it because any form of protection has to be a good thing. My issue was that these unscrupulous pharma-type companies were getting fat off the back of this issue, and people were falling for it. Most of the time, it just takes sensible hygiene and very little else to keep germs at bay. I think even experts agree that before the advent of the anti-bac, hospitals were kept clean by constantly wiping surfaces and maintaining a high level of cleanliness; if they didn't get all the germs, they would come back but would be wiped down again with soap and water before they had a chance to take hold. Since then, it seems that cleaners felt that a quick wipe down with some gloop would be perfectly sufficient, not considering the idea that if you don't get all the bacteria, it will come back stronger. The act of washing hands was the most significant contributor to arresting the development of the bugs, not the anti-bacterial qualities of pharmaceutical gloop.

Now we come to masks. I can't wear the damned things. Ever since I was a young child, I have not been able to cover my head with a blanket when lying in bed. I don't think it is claustrophobia, or if it is, it is the mildest form. I would just start to hyperventilate. Anything that restricts free airflow has this effect. I do have other issues with these things as well. I get that, in the beginning, when we were trying to restrict the virus, if we had to go into enclosed spaces, this was an effective way of doing things. But only to a point. In a building where there is no wind, the virus will drop out very quickly after exhaling unless you sneeze or cough which was where the whole thing became an issue. In the open, the wind could keep it airborne almost indefinitely or take it out of harm's way quickly. So the idea that masks outside were of no use never held water, and the idea that wearing masks inside, even if you never came near anyone else, was equally ill-thought-out. Since the virus has become less severe, I believe that masks have become counterproductive. When we exhale, we don't just exhale deoxygenated air. It is one of the methods that the body uses to get rid of things it does want to be hanging around inside. This is primarily infections of the various flavours, but also other things as well. We have survived through the millennia by using this method very nicely, thank you. So why would it have changed now? The problem with masks is that they trap all this foreign gunk on the inside of the mask. When you breathe in, the air comes through the mask and dislodges the gunk from the mask, so it gets sucked straight back into the system that has just rejected it. This can't be healthy. The other issue I have is, with my very basic knowledge of how the body works, I know that a strong immune system requires an active immune system. If we take the work away from what our bodies are designed to do, then the immune system will just say, 'Fine, I'm not needed. I'll just sit here and do the crossword and let the pharma companies do all the hard work.' Then one day, when the body suddenly doesn't have the benefit of Pfizer or Astra Zeneca to do its job, it finds itself unprepared. It is a sad fact that we need to breathe this stuff in to keep our bodies functioning efficiently. I don't think the pharma industry, the medical industry or the government will ever agree with this statement, as it is too big a money-making industry, but it doesn't make it any less true.

Measures

During the entire process, there were some measures that some took that were not well thought out. One or two turned out to be for the better, but not many. Here are some of my favourites.

St. Johns Park in South Wimbledon. Now, let me set the scene. This park is around about, but not more than one acre. It is part of St John's Church grounds and runs alongside the main road that goes between South Wimbledon and Morden in southwest London. There is a small one-way street forming a boundary to the north and a larger dual carriageway forming a border to the south. There are two entrances/exits, one at each of these two road junctions. There is a path that runs around the outer limits of the inside of the park, and the entire park is fenced off. Between the fence and the road, there is a paved footway that is quite narrow. Just enough room to get two people side-by-side. In all the years I have known this park – and that is going into decades – I have never known there to be more than six people in the park at any one time, including me and anyone else I was with, so it is not exactly overrun. There is not much to it. What it did do was to provide a more pleasant route for the short distance between the two gates to the paved footpath. It was not a shortcut, just slightly more pleasant, and one did not have to negotiate their way around other pedestrians coming towards you. Lockdown then came along, and some bright spark decided that locking one gate – with no warning at the other gate that this had been done – was a really good idea. What it meant was that you would go into the park and walk to the exit, only to find that you had to turn around, make your way back then squeeze past the pedestrians on the pavement outside. They didn't want to stop people going into the park. They only wanted to herd people into the smallest possible area, ensuring a nice, even spread of the disease. Instead of a perfectly natural way of creating 'social distancing', they ensured that everyone had to do the exact opposite. Good thinking, batman!

The next one is my local DIY. I won't give them the oxygen of publicity, and I'm sure all of them had similar ways of dealing with the issues. This particular one is a large place on two levels, with parking on both levels. Before 2020, they had one staffed till and four self-service checkouts on each floor. There were two staff members on each floor assigned to the checkouts. So that allowed ten people at any one time dealing with the purchasing of their items, all being looked after by four staff members. Post-lockdown, they changed everything. The self-checkouts were removed, and staffed tills were put in their place. This exists to the present day. Although there were three on each floor, bar one occasion, I only ever saw one person staffing the tills on each floor. Customers then had to queue for service. Many people don't like self-checkout tills as they see it as taking jobs away from ordinary people. Unfortunately, on this occasion, there appeared to be fewer staff than before – normally two people, one on each floor. Their policy had the effect of having people standing close to each other queuing (2 metres apparently) for sometimes as long as half an hour. Before 2020, I never saw a queue of anything more than one customer. Now there are always queues that are seldom less than five people. How is this helping with social distancing? Surely, if they could get through checkout quicker, it would be a lot healthier. Now we have to stand breathing over everyone else for 30 minutes, thereby ensuring a nice even spread of the disease. It has to be better for the store, the public and the government to go back to the original plan. Nice one, Batman!

Our local recycling centre is another one. This is a place where twelve cars can park up and deal with their recycling. The area open to the public is probably three acres, and it is all outside. There were never more than 20 or so people there at any one time in addition to the staff. Despite this, the council decided that they needed to restrict numbers even more than this by introducing a booking system. There is no problem with social distancing in a place this size. All this has done was to cause an epidemic of fly-tipping because people couldn't wait three months for a slot. When the restrictions were lifted, the entire population descended on the centre. This caused tailbacks almost a mile long. The problem with this was that the queues went into a fairly narrow residential road, and the locals couldn't get out of their own driveways. When they could, they couldn't get out of the street without having to join the queue even though they weren't going to the centre. They re-introduced the booking procedures and the problems were solved. I just think that if they hadn't introduced the restrictions in the first place, it would never have snowballed. The fact that it had, meant they had to take action, and, in my opinion, that action was measured and appropriate.

There were plenty of road restrictions that made no sense, like forcing vehicles into narrower roads by closing off one lane to favour or encourage cyclists. It didn't. It was never going to. All it did was to cause traffic jams where none needed to exist. Another one was to restrict all but public service vehicles from one particular town centre in South London. Sounds fine until you realise that the traffic was diverted past a junior school and a high school, causing traffic jams in these locations at the time when pupils were attending school. Well done, Batman, you are really doing well here.

It concerns me that even at the end of 2022, people are still believing that another lockdown would be a good thing. This is despite the fact that we have seen how China dealt with it. They locked its population down for two entire years believing that the virus would give up, pack its bags and walk off into the sunset. What actually happened was that it just went to sleep until conditions improved, then carried on. At the time of writing, China has got a problem on its hands.

People in the rest of the world are still getting the virus, but the population are better protected and are coping. China's population is not. As long as they sort themselves out, the only lesson I can take is that, while I'm aware that it has not gone away, it is no more threatening than influenza, so lockdown doesn't work, and a robust immune system does. We can see this in the children who were born during the lockdown. I have heard stories of kids that are getting ill at the drop of a hat. They just need to walk past someone with a cold and they are sniffling away for weeks. It isn't spoken about much, but these kids weren't playing outside, getting their knees dirty and doing the sort of stuff that kids do. Because of that, their immune system hasn't had the opportunity to develop properly. Don't get me wrong, the initial lockdown was needed. We did not have the tools to deal with the issue, and the virus had to be controlled when it first arrived, but these measures should only be used in very specific circumstances and there needs to be a clearly defined goal.

The second lockdown was a very bad joke. If you are going to lock down, you have to lock down. You can't tell people that you have to stay indoors unless your geraniums look a little sad, in which case you are free to trail around garden centres all you like. We had a system where a person, during the lockdown, could go onto a tube train, alight and go into a supermarket, pick things up and put them back down, cough on all the produce, then stroll down the road to the garden centre and breathe on everyone and everything en route, but you couldn't pop into a pub on the way home for a swift half, because that would be too dangerous. When you could, you had to remain seated as if the virus only spread at an altitude of 5' off the ground. I do not believe for a moment that the second lockdown did anything other than tell the public that the government were responding. It didn't have to be an effective response, just a response. So, no lockdown. If they are going to have a strategy, use the three rules that I always went by: It has to be affordable, timely, and it must have a specific achievable aim. This must be made clear from the outset. Initially, we needed to try to limit its spread while the boffins sought a cure. They have found one and are constantly developing it as the virus mutates. A lockdown strategy would not be able to use this same strategy, and I can't think of any other reason.

Ditch the mask, I say. If you are ill, don't go to work. Put pressure on governments and industry to endorse this. When I was a young copper, it was a disciplinary offence to come to work with an infectious condition other than an infectious personality. Now it is expected. Companies want productivity whether or not the individual is in a fit state to deliver, and they don't seem to care that other people could be infected because they would expect them to work through their ailments. It is wrong, and it shouldn't happen. If we are sensible, there shouldn't be that many issues. People will still get ill. People will still die. It is the nature of life. Protecting ourselves without regard for the welfare of everyone else isn't the way to do it. Nor is protecting our profits at the expense of other people's health.

THE ENVIRONMENT

Apparently there is a conversation out there about the environment. You'd never know, hardly a whisper from anyone. Except of course environmentalists, who think that we should all stop doing everything or the planet will die in the next fortnight. We should go nowhere, do nothing, eat only grass and only breathe if absolutely necessary. Then we have the media who only want to sell copy and therefore believe that doom and gloom is the way forward and that the general population are too stupid to think for themselves. Oh, and politicians. They are also in there. Can't be a politician unless you are making decisions about things that you have little knowledge of and couldn't control even if you did. Then you have everyone else who would wade into the conversations that are being held in our pubs, coffee houses and everywhere else.

Who am I forgetting...? Oh yes, scientists. But what do they know? They have only had a lifetime of studying the subject. Going to the affected places, taking samples looking at habits of life on earth. But they aren't campaigners, so the environmentalists aren't going to take what they are saying seriously unless they are on their message. Nor are they trying to sell newspapers, so the media are going to side-line them unless they are on their message. They are certainly not politicians but they have to give these politicians their study results only to see them redacted into whatever message the politicians want the public to hear.

So hardly anyone is talking about it apart from the entire population. With that comes the inevitable differences of opinion about why it is happening and what the most effective way of solving the problem is. It doesn't help that scientists aren't in agreement. If they aren't then who else can be. What happens is that those that espouse a particular theory will seek out the scientists who agree with them and claim that their views are irrefutable... while someone on the next table down is busy refuting it with their own irrefutable scientific data. I don't know who is right. All I know is that something is happening out there. The wheels have been set in motion and it may well be too late to stop it now. The earth's climate has been fluctuating since the day it was born and will continue. It would be good if we didn't exacerbate the issue. In the meantime, campaigners, the media and politicians – both bar room and actual politicians – will try to convince us that their way is the only way.

Farming

Let us take farming for the first of my targets. The population of this planet is going up rapidly. With that comes the need to feed them. Farmers are having to produce more and more food to satisfy this ever-increasing number of mouths. Intensive farming is everywhere and it is devastating to our environment. And here is how... I think. Vegans will have us believe that animal husbandry is causing methane to get into our air and this is the primary cause of the impending disaster that is the ever-growing hole in the ozone layer. But is it. I am going to try to pick this argument apart. We can start with the fact that there are fewer bovine animals in the world now than there have been for thousands of years. Herds of buffalo in Africa and bison in the Americas tens of thousands strong roamed the earth right up until humans started wiping them out. You'd be lucky to see a herd of more than a hundred in any one place these days. Their population is a very small proportion of what it was. The same goes for antelopes and deer. We can't just take domestic cows in isolation, they are all part of the environment and we are now left with a small fraction of them. Domestic cows, in the past made up a relatively small proportion of the bovine population. There may well be more domestic cows now, but not so much that it has made up for the loss of wild ones. So if cows are such a big problem now, why weren't they before. And if they were

298

before, it stands to reason that the problem they cause are less now because there are fewer of the animals.

Then we take a closer look and these emissions. Cows fart and burp, we can't control that. They eat grass and their digestive system produces the stuff. It has to go somewhere and that is out. Some of that emission is methane. Much of it drops out and goes into the soil. This is good as nitrogen enriches the earth. Most of it mixes with the atmosphere and a tiny proportion gets into the ozone. That is not good. What I am saying, is don't believe that when a cow lets rip, the whole lot is methane and it all buys a one-way ticket to the ozone layer and sits there watching the planet slowly heat up. It's more complex than that. We also need to understand that cows don't just release gaseous waste. Solids come out as well. These also enrich the soil and keep the ecosystem that is always busy underneath the surface alive. It isn't just livestock; it is all animals. They contribute as much as they take out. I am aware that some farming methods are less than humane and I would prefer that this was stopped, but I don't think it is as big a contributor to the environmental problems as some would have us believe. I think they help more than they hinder.

What about the idea that if we stopped farming cows, there would be fewer cows in the world. That doesn't work on any level. It may be true that the cows are reproducing more than is natural due to the farming methods employed in our modern world, but whatever they produce falls fowl to the slaughterer's axe, so their life expectancy was considerably shorter than those that are not farmed. A subsistence farmer that owns thirty cows that he is breeding for the meat industry, will have thirty cows thirty years later. The guy that has thirty cows in a field and is left to their own devices and is not used in any way in the human food chain, will have too many to support in the same field thirty years on. They would have produced fewer calves per cow each year, but few would have died early, so they would be free to breed to their heart's content for many more years.

My concern with farming is cereal and vegetable crops. While vegans are preaching about the disaster caused by animal farming, they forget about this side of it. For the last 50 or so years, the insect population has been in steady decline. This is a direct result of insecticides and other pesticides (I don't like that word). They are used to increase yield by controlling diseases and animals that feed on the plants. The stripping back of hedgerows to make way for more farming land reduces the habitat that the animals live in, be they hedgehogs, rabbits or insects, bugs and worms. It isn't the livestock farmers that are doing this. They may be using a little poison in the cattle barns, but they aren't spraying entire ecosystems and they aren't destroying hedgerows where the insects live. There is a quarter of these hedgerows in this country now than there was in the 1960s. People used to complain that at certain times of the year, their cars were splattered with insects while driving through the countryside. Now you would find hardly any on your car. This shows just how much the insect population has declined. An old Indian sage once said that if we took out all the insects on the planet, life on earth would die out within six months. If we destroyed worms, bacteria and all the microbial creatures, it would be more like six weeks. If we were to get rid of the human population, life would proliferate. Trees would grow through the structures we have built. Animals would repopulate towns and cities. Pollution would become a thing of the past – except for methane, that could be a problem. So don't underestimate the importance of our insects.

These crop farmers are not rotating crops or leaving land fallow to revitalise the soil for a few years either. Probably because they can't afford to as the people need more food. What this means is that whatever crop they are growing is drawing out all the nutrients and nothing is replacing it. Farmers have to use artificial fertilisers to grow anything. A study some years ago showed that vegetables today, when compared with those from the

1960s had at best sixty percent of the vitamins and minerals and in some cases – particularly iron – up to ten percent. If you think that is not good for us, think about the worms and insects that enrich our soils. They aren't getting what they need either.

If this all seems like I am just having a pop at vegans, I am not. Eat what you like, it doesn't bother me. What I am having a go at is the message that we are getting from them. In my view, their message, that we should all be eating vegetables only, is inaccurate. What is best is balance. The human digestive system can survive on vegetables alone, but it is more efficient at digesting and drawing nutrients from meat products. Humans throughout history have eaten whatever is available. Those that live near the sea have had a more pescatarian diet while those that lived inland tended away from fish. Those that lived in areas where animals were scarce tended towards a more vegetable-based diet. We, in the world in which we live, have access to whatever we want, whenever we want it. We have a choice. Some choose vegan or vegetarian some choose a more varied, omnivorous diet and some are more carnivorous. None of us are wrong so please don't be judgemental, especially when your argument doesn't stack up.

As a caveat to me not having a pop, I think I can have a pop at pescatarians. At least those who only eat fish as they don't like the idea of eating cute little lambs and calves. There may be people out there who need to adjust their diet for medical reasons, for example. So I won't judge all. Firstly, if you think we shouldn't eat meat because all living things should be allowed to live their lives, remember that fish is meat, and they are living things. Just because they are not gambolling in a meadow does not mean they have any less right. Secondly, no living thing on earth has any more of a right to live than anything else. All living things get eaten by something at some point. Thirdly, plants are also living things. From an environmental point of view, we are overfishing our seas and that is a much bigger issue than cows' flatulence. An unhealthy ocean is an unhealthy planet. So please don't believe that, like vegans are claiming, you are being environmentally friendly. You are not.

Pollution

Never mind flatulent cows, what about flatulent motor vehicles. In 2023 London, we have been told that we have to pay to drive polluters in town. This is a money grab to pay for the other Ultra Low Emmision Zone (ULEZ) policies that do make a difference and nothing more. The ULEZ itself policy isn't the problem. There are plenty of policies that aren't leaching money from people who really can't afford it. The electrification of taxis and buses for example but there is so much more they can do and charging people will make no difference other than to make it an elite activity for the wealthy only. No one drives in London unless they either have no choice, or they don't have to worry about parking and traffic jams and don't care about the cost. It is not about the congestion charge – which has done nothing to ease congestion – or the ULEZ charge. It is about lack of parking, badly designed streets, too many roadworks that are in place for too long. This and a whole load of other issues. Plumbers, electricians, builders and so many other people have to have a vehicle to carry tools and equipment that you physically could not carry on public transport. Furniture removers, food lorries, transport companies need access to London. All these people have to drive in London and most have vehicles that are not compliant, so they just pass the costs onto to their customers. That means we have to pay the charge even if we aren't driving. Your average independent tradesman cannot afford £60 000 for an electric vehicle and even if they could, there wouldn't be sufficient charging stations to cope. The derisory £2000 they are offering to scrap vehicles that are worth £30 000 is not worth the paper it's written on.

The biggest polluters are Lorries and Aircraft. We can ban them tomorrow as long as you don't mind having no tourism in or out of London. We would also have to have no food in the shops, no clothes in Next and Top Shop. No furniture delivered to our houses – The DFL sale would have to come to an end, now that would be something – no building materials to build new or repair old houses, and no fuel in the Petrol stations. Not that it would matter, there wouldn't be any vehicles to use them. We can't electrify these huge trucks and aircraft – although tech is being developed in this area – at the moment as the battery packs would be as big as the lorries themselves so they wouldn't have any room for cargo. That may raise issues of them being pointless.

Boris Johnson wanted to build an airport in the Thames estuary. He was lambasted for this idea. Environmentalist said that it would destroy the wildlife of the area. Politicians said it would be too expensive and everyone didn't give it a moment's thought. If they had done this, the current airport could have been rewilded cancelling, or at least mitigating the environmentalist argument. Politicians never seem to worry about costs when it is their idea. My main point is that the pollution would never come straight into London, it would be out in the North Sea. There would be a fraction of the traffic in the area of the current airport, so pollution would come down sharply from that source as well. There would be plenty of down sides, but that is the nature of air travel. If you are going to have it, you accept the consequences. It doesn't mean you can't mitigate them. One could argue pros and cons until we are blue in the face, there are always going to be problems. The question to answer is, are those problems going to be more or less than those that we endure now.

So if our new ULEZ charge is going to make any difference, it will only be to force those who don't have to go through London, to go the long way around it. This will necessitate hitting the M25. That would clog up that system even more than it is now causing more pollution which will be blown into London anyway. How about some other ideas. If you don't want to divert aircraft, what about sorting out the road works in London. On the rare occasion that I drive in this town, I will come across at least four road works where there are temporary traffic lights for every trip. Of these four, you'd be lucky to find any with active work going on. The works are going on for too long and causing traffic build up. Near my home a small bridge collapsed causing a major thoroughfare to be closed for thirty months. The original collapse was due to lack of maintenance. The secondary collapse was entirely the fault of intransigent local politicians wanting to do it cheaper rather than listen to these noisome experts. So the ensuing 30 months of delays could only be laid at their door. It was two years before we, the residents, were informed that they were actively looking for a contractor to take on the work. That is two years of nothing. Two years of traffic jams. The delay was probably down to them searching for another expert who could rewrite the advice to make it look like it wasn't their fault. This was no more than a small tunnel under the road to allow a small river to flow though. If you want to sort out emissions, sort out that sort of thing.

Maybe look at the 20mph speed limit. I have to drive in third gear to maintain that speed. I can go to fourth gear to keep 30mph and fifth to go to 40mph. At each speed in each gear, the car is using the same amount of power. This means that my car will use twice as much fuel at 20mph than it does at 40 to go the same distance. More fuel, more emissions, more emissions, more climate change. There are so many other things they can do to bolster the ULEZ policies. The one that makes no positive impact is charging working class, struggling London workers. All it does is improve the mayoral coffers. Sadiq Khan – man of the people (as long as the 'people' are fabulously wealthy and don't clutter up the road like those nasty poor people).

There are other issues. If ULEZ charging did help in the centre of London, then extending it would mean that those who Live in the Greater London area and drove outside the previous zone to avoid the charge would now have no problem in going into the old boundaries as they are already being charged anyway. This could mean increased traffic in the more congested areas. This is hypothetical as I don't believe it will make any difference. What about the guy who decides to visit London and comes by car as it is the cheapest and quickest way to do it. I have seen that those people would come into London but then go home the same day rather than stay few days longer, all to avoid a second ULEZ charge. What this means is that pubs, restaurants, shops and every other sphere of business loses out. Add to that the fact that the vehicle will have done the same mileage coming into and going out of the charging zone, and therefore the same emissions whether they stayed two hours or two days. Another issue is the same for all these charges, including the congestion charge. There is no evidence to show that the actual charge – whichever one you want to target – has had what the politicians have stated is the effect that they seek. What it has meant is that the political machine has another source of income that they will not be able to do without. Not only that, they will not want traffic to be reduced, because that would mean their new income source would be diminished. So from the political side of it, it could have the opposite effect on traffic management.

At this point in time, life as we know it would be made more difficult without the motor vehicles. We cannot operate without lorries to transport food, building materials and all our daily needs to us. The electric vehicles are not as environmentally friendly as some politicians would have us believe. They may have fewer emissions on the road, but the electricity has to come from somewhere and it isn't all renewables, we simply do not have enough of that to go around. The batteries have a shelf life and no one has publicly tackled the question of how we dispose of the used ones. I'm told that they can be used to store electricity, but that is limited in terms of time and space. How are they going to be disposed of safely?

It gets worse. Never mind that the cars are made primarily of plastics. The batteries aren't just plastic either. They have amongst other things, lithium and cobalt in them. The environmental and socio-economic disaster that is being caused by mining these minerals is being brushed over by everyone. These minerals are found in many of the poorer drier countries of the world where human rights are an inconvenience best ignored. The miners are diverting precious water resources away from where it is needed in the villages in order to feed the thirsty mines.

The local population are being uprooted to make way for these multicorporate fat-cats and the village men used as little more than slave labour. All so Ms Fortescue-Smythe can have a trendy electric car bought for her by rich daddy. And what happens when that resource runs dry? Whose lives are we going to destroy for the next miracle mineral that is going to solve the worlds energy wants? If we are all going to get high and mighty about environmental issues, consider the impact outside your own little sphere. You may find the impact is worse than we had in the past.

The Genertion Game

Let us now move onto to our young Swedish campaigner who is making all sorts of noises about this. When she started, it was from the heart stuff. Perhaps a little ill-informed, but from the heart nevertheless. They were issues that she believed in. Now I am not so sure. I think oil and energy companies are writing her scripts and bankrolling her campaign. It all seems very well thought out at first but consider what is being said and what the reality is. Greta Thunberg has a message, but this message is seldom argued. It just appears that she is standing there, having a rant then disappearing before the awkward questions come.

310

Apparently my generation ruined her life and all the lives of her generation. Really? Let's look at that.

As a young man, when I went shopping, I put the purchased goods into a cardboard box. This box came from the shop who were asking us to reuse boxes that delivered stuff to their store. So no plastics and recycling before recycling was a thing.

When I bought veggies, they were, more often than not, loose, and if they were covered, it was a single layer of paper or plastic. Not this ridiculous system where they cover the goods in plastic, then protect the plastic by covering it in plastic. Then they put all of that in a plastic bag. Why?

We had our milk delivered in a milk float that was driven by an electric motor. We recycled our milk bottles by leaving them out for the milkman to collect and reuse when he made his delivery. The bottles were glass not plastic. It wasn't just milk bottles. Where I lived as a child, you paid a deposit on bottles of pop and beer and suchlike. This meant that you took them back to get your money back instead of filling up plastic bin liners with empty bottles or just abandoning them on the street.

I recall that the only bottles that we didn't pay a deposit on were small 250ml beer bottles. Strangely, these were the only bottles we saw littering the streets. In the home, we had three plug points in the lounge – one for the TV, one for the radio and one for the vacuum cleaner. There were two in the kitchen. The oven was wired into the mains, so all you needed was one for the fridge and one for any electric implements. Then there was one in each room for the vacuum cleaner. There were no extension leads, no multi-plug adapters, nothing like that because there wasn't anything else to plug in. The tv service only started at 5.30pm, so it was the radio or you found something else to do during the day. If something broke down, it would be fixed as a first option and replaced only if absolutely necessary. Don't get me wrong, we still had waste, but it was one bin for a family of six. Now I have four bins outside my house for the two of us and I don't consider myself wasteful at all.

If I wanted to go anywhere as a youngster growing up in Africa, it was bicycle or shank's pony. The car was for commuting (no public transport to speak of where I lived), family outings and shopping. Aircraft journeys were virtually unheard of in my family. Even when I arrived in England it was all about public transport or bicycle.

Do we think that millennials and generation X are blameless, and it is all on my generation? I think not. This is an age where everyone demands that everything is at their fingertips. They lift their eyes to the heavens when they hear us banging on about having to be patient and not expecting everything. We live in an age where all the youngsters who are complaining about us, have computers, mobile phones gaming consuls, headphones and electronic gizmos literally coming out of their ears. Everything is available at the press of a plastic button and delivered to the house wrapped up in three layers of plastic all in a cardboard box that is taped up with yards of plastic tape and placed in another box for no apparent reason. Our schools are clogged with traffic at the beginning and end of the school day because our precious little darlings couldn't possibly walk for fear of being run over by all the cars taking the other sprogs to school. We have food from anywhere in the world at our fingertips with no idea of how it gets to us. If the parents allowed their kids to use public transport, that was akin to child neglect. Their clothes have to be 'labelled' and the family car needed to not embarrass them.

It is a consumer's world where everything has to be consumed all the time in order to give themselves to energy to whinge about me destroying their planet. I'm not saying that we are blameless, I'm just saying look in the mirror occasionally and perhaps dial it down a little. And don't be an ungrateful little brat like our cuddly little Greta.

So, climate change is happening we are told. No shit sherlock! The climate has always been changing. It has been in a state of flux since the year dot. To me, nature is at work all the time. It is constantly trying to maintain a balance. If something upsets the balance, it does something to sort it out. A little pestilence here and there, the odd war maybe even a meteorite to shake things up a little and when it gets too much, a quick ice age. This is the Earth's reset button. Its equivalent of turning the computer off and then back on again. I don't believe we are causing the change. I think we may be exacerbating it, but the earth will get its own way in the end. We certainly aren't going to mitigate anything until India, China, Russia and the USA get their combined acts together and help us out a little. I don't see that happening so charging people for ULEZ isn't going to do anything outside clogging up the mayoral coffers with too much cash. I would much rather allow the bottom of my garden to grow a little wild to encourage insects, grow some veg, allow other animals the space to live their lives and just be decent and hope everyone else does the same. Perhaps eat a little more meat so that you fart less – good for the environment.

SHADOWY FIGURES

This is where I reassert that I have no party-political allegiance. To my mind, the idea that some politicians' ideas are right or wrong because they are of a particular political hue is ludicrous. I hear it all the time. If the Tory party say they are going to raise the tax threshold, that means you don't have to pay tax under a certain amount. The Tories will say that this will mean poorer people paying less tax, which is good. The supporters of every other party say the threshold is applicable to the rich as well, and they don't need it. They will also say it is underhanded, right-wing policies that have made it so that they have no choice. When they increase taxes for the wealthy, the wealthy people just pass the losses onto the general public. When they lower them, they are pandering to their cronies. If the labour party want to bring back some industries into public ownership, they will say that this prevents wealthy people from profiteering off poorer people when supplying vital services. The Tories will say the opponents of private ownership are stifling competition and forcing entrepreneurs to look to other countries to create wealth. The poorer people then lose employment opportunities. The fact is that if the idea is a good idea coming from a good place, then it's a good idea. It matters not who came up with it. Let's face it; there aren't any new ideas in politics. It's all rehashed,

315

remarketed and regurgitated to the (un)suspecting public. The biggest problem is not the decisions that are made; it's the execution of the policies created by the decisions.

I do look at politics from a distance, and I think I can spot a trend emerging. I hope you enjoy what follows. It may be entirely true or completely false. I don't know, nor do I care. In fact, the truth, as always, probably sits quite comfortably somewhere in the middle. What follows may seem somewhat anti-democratic, but we have to understand that we don't elect Prime Ministers; we elect our own local MPs and the party with the most elected members, wins. The party leader is then top Johnny-banana and gets to call themselves PM. The PM does not run the country per se, but he or she does get to choose the cabinet of ministers who do.

The Tory hierarchy – and by this I don't mean the ones that we, the public, see on a daily basis, more the ones in the shadowy recesses that no one sees – like to try to identify potential leaders from a very early age and groom them to high office. It doesn't always work, I don't think they expected Thatcher in a thousand years, but it is a tried and tested method. While it may not be good for the people of this country, it has undoubtedly always worked for those who pull the strings. I will also say that the Labour also do this on a smaller scale. They are still a little wet behind the ears compared to their older antagonists, so they are still learning the ropes.

To this end, David – I've misplaced my spine – Cameron was bound to have been in their sights. The right school, the right university and a little nudge here and there, and he could turn out to be quite malleable. The Labour are in power. They have swept into power under a Tory party in disarray and imploding on itself, so they don't look like they are going to be shifted any time soon. Not too much of a problem, so many of Blair's policies are the same ones the Tories would want in place so they don't have to work too hard in parliament. A few murmurs of discontent at PMQs just to make it look like there is an opposition but not too much. They can use this period to regroup. They have time.

Tony Blair, when he was premier, decided that he was there to make the decisions. Especially about membership of the European union, a subject that had started to rumble and was steadily gaining momentum. Towards the end of his tenure, he didn't care what the general public thought. He was elected to make decisions, so he was going to make them. Never mind all this "of the people, by the people, for the people" bollox. My parliament, my rules! But the dissenting voices were getting louder, and he was losing support. By the end, he was, in his eyes, heading for a drubbing at the ballad box, so he cut and ran, handing over the sinking ship together with an economy in tatters and a party in disarray to Gordon Brown. A poisoned challis if ever there was one.

The Tories, sensing a certain victory in the next election, dumped their ineffectual leader, IDS, who, after all, was only holding the keys while they found a suitable replacement. This was the ideal time for Cameron. They had been grooming him for all they were worth for years waiting for an opportunity, and this was it. Anyone could have won the next election over the FUBAR that was Labour. Cameron was duly selected to lead the party. This party then went on to win the general election, albeit an unconvincing win forcing them into a coalition with the LibDems. The narrowness of the victory should have been a big red-flag warning to our shadowy backroom politicians. As an aside, it made Brown the first Prime Minister since Douglas-Home to never win an election campaign as PM. (Truss has one over on him. She never won or lost a campaign as PM).

There follows a period where Cameron bumbles along trying to get his pet projects through the haze of coalition government indecision. As much as people hated Clegg for throwing in his lot with the Tories, I think it probably mitigated much of the more right-wing policies espoused by Cameron and his party. Many people get on their high horses about Clegg but let's face it, if you are the leader of a political party, then you have ambitions. If you are in a party who, in the current political climate, is destined, forever, to be an also-ran, then wouldn't you grasp the opportunity for you and some of your closer colleagues to be at the centre of government? Even if you are no more than a thorn in their side. And those who believe that he should have stuck with some of his more liberal policies, consider what would have happened if he had fought that losing battle. One has to maintain some authority and stymying the Tories' more odious policies is one way to make your presence felt. Fighting battles that are already lost can only do harm.

Throughout this period, rumblings about our membership of the European union are still getting newspaper column inches and it is becoming increasingly evident that the public are going to make decisions based on this one issue. Cameron starts to make noises. He is clearly wanting to remain in the union, but his primary concern is remaining at No 10. He makes a few well publicised visits to Europe to put across the concerns. The commission sends him away with his tail between his legs each time. He then tells one and all that he will continue to try and get assurances from the commission but if this does not succeed, then he will give the people of Britain their voice in a referendum.

This is his campaign pledge for the approaching general election. He wants to win this properly and divest himself of the millstone that is the LibDems. Although he maintains that he would campaign to remain in the union, he believes that by appearing to listen to the public, he could achieve his aim.

He wins the election with an overall majority, and, shock of shocks, he keeps his promise and sorts out a referendum. The ensuing campaign was a strange affair, and I couldn't help but think those people in the shadows pulling all the strings were at work. I had to ask myself why a group of people whose job it is to debate failed so completely to debate anything. The 'leavers' had a strategy that was to keep it positive and simple. 'It's all going to be so much better out of the Union,' 'We will have control of our destiny,' 'We are going to be richer, better, blah, blah'. No one really believed the rhetoric, but everything was positive. On the other hand, the remainers remained negative. They only argued against what the leavers were saying, putting a negative spin on anything they said while suggesting that leave supporters were unintelligent, anti-Europe, racist bigots. That's going to win votes now, isn't it?

Through all of this, Labour is being run by Jeremy Corbyn. He was a godsend to the Tory puppeteers. A man of principle. A man who was an independent thinker. I had some hopes for him. British politics has not had an effective opposition since Neil Kinnock... possibly, in the early eighties or possibly even Michael Foot before him. Corbyn was the only person who seemed willing to step up and oppose policies. Unfortunately, his area of expertise was being a thorn on the side of leadership whether it was his own party or any other. He was never a leader and so he was an easy target for career politicians, especially those politicians who operate in the shadows and never have to justify their decisions to the public. The one thing that was clear was that he was not keen on the European system and was therefore a leaver. He could never say that out loud as he had to toe the party line. This is not what he was put onto this planet to do, so he was not convincing.

What this meant was that the Labour party, as a strong supporter of remaining in Europe had a leader who could not state that he supported Europe, because he didn't. Nor could he support the leave campaign because that wasn't the labour position. The leave campaign within the Tory Party latched onto that as did the remainers. So he got it from all sides. The coup-de-grâce for all sides was the ant-Semitism row. I do not for a moment believe that Corbyn was antisemitic. I think this was just the Jewish right-wing contingent of these shadowy figures, poisoning

321

the waters to reduce his credibility (this may seem anti-Semitic, but it isn't, it is anti-right-wing Jewish fundamentalism). He was a supporter of the Palestinian cause and did not like the Israeli policies on Palestine, but that does not make him anti-Semitic, just anti-war and possibly anti-Zionist. The Labour hierarchy just got scared and succumbed to the bullying tactics employed by his antagonists. I saw the interview with him on TV when the interviewer was trying to get Corbyn to apologise for antisemitism in the Labour Party. The interviewer should hang his head in shame. It was an example of the worst kind of journalism.

The interviewer kept on asking the same question knowing full well that Corbyn could not answer it in any way that he could be happy that his honesty had not been compromised. The question (paraphrased) – "This is your opportunity to apologise for the anti Semitism in your party, will you do that?" – was put to him in that way for that very reason. If Corbyn were to have said, 'Okay, I apologise for this antisemitism', the media would have jumped on this regardless of how he phrased it and proclaimed that the Labour Party was a seething mass of Jew-hating National Socialists – which is clearly not true. He couldn't do that. Nor could he say, 'There are no antisemites in the Labour Party to apologise for.' There probably are some in the party, but no more than anywhere else in any other organisation in the country – and remember, being pro-Palestinian is not the same as being anti-Semitic. Yes, he would have to weed out those who were identifiably antisemitic wherever he could and have a policy to prevent these people from having a position of prominence. Had he said there weren't any, he would then have been accused of denying a problem exists. All they would need to do is find evidence against one person, and Corbyn's argument would crumble. He therefore had no choice but to not answer the demands of this really bad piece of media hype. Because it frightened the Labour hierarchy, they have opted to replace Corbin for a damp squib who will probably be our PM after the election. I have had trouble finding staunch labour supporters who like the prospect. Hopefully, he will do better than the limp-wristed, ineffectual way he led the Department of Public Prosecutions. That is something I would brush over on my CV if I were in his position.

This half-hearted debate on our membership of the EU was carried out and went the way of Brexit. The now completely metaphorically invertebrate Cameron got the hell in and walked away from the whole mess. Now our shadowy puppeteers had a challenge. They needed a replacement. Whoever got the job would be demonised, unpopular and doomed to failure. They would have to negotiate their way around a decision that is not supported by, as near as makes no difference, half the population of the country and a considerably higher proportion of politicians. None of whom are ever going to be convinced otherwise. Another poisoned chalice. They therefore did not want one of their 'chosen ones' to get the job. Rather, find a fall guy who will do all the things that needed to be done and keep their Golden boys – for they are invariably boys – out of the unwanted limelight. They weren't worried about elections. The Labour Party didn't want this particular chalice until someone else had taken the metaphorical poison then waited until they had choked on it, All they would have to do is wait until the dust had settled. Enter Theresa-the fall-guy-May. She could have been the Angel Gabriel himself, come to sprinkle fairy dust throughout the country; it wouldn't have made a jot of difference. Nothing she was ever going to do was going to be good enough. The people who had now joined the 'remoaners' club were going to scrutinise every syllable and trash everything, regardless of the efficacy of any decisions made.

She went into the office with a comfortable majority and decided that she didn't want that. She went back to the polls to be able to tell everyone that she had a personal mandate to do what she wanted. Didn't work very well, but she had got through that spectacularly bad decision albeit without an effective majority. She set out to get

324

through the quagmire of the first couple of years of Brexit negotiations. Nothing went particularly well. European leaders were not going to negotiate anything. They were not interested in the democratic process we went through; they just wanted to make sure that no one else had the same idea. Given that Europe at this time was sliding distinctly toward the right of the political spectrum, this shouldn't come as a surprise.

May had done her job and taken the major blows on the chin. It was time for her to go and let proper politicians – one with the correct set of genitalia – carry the baton. Our puppeteers had been hard at work in the background working on the next leader. There really wasn't much to choose from. Boris Johnson was a bumbling buffoon, but a bumbling buffoon who was a consummate campaigner. He had convinced people that blue was green throughout the Brexit campaign. He had won two terms as London Mayor and, as bad as he was, came away with a lasting legacy. It doesn't matter who started the 'Borisbike' phenomenon; when all is said and done, they were called Boris bikes. He did get rid of those ridiculous bendy buses. They were perfect for cities with wide streets and not too much traffic, but not London. Then, of course, we have the Boris Buses as well. Like him or hate him, his PR team are top-notch.

This is the guy that will win us the next election, they said. We don't want him making any actual decisions. That would be a disaster. He can just win a campaign, stay in place for a reasonable period, and then go away and live his life. This, of course, was not the Bozza way. Once he had won the election, he started having fun. Yes, he was caught lying through his back teeth several times, but he didn't illegally invade a sovereign state as Blair did. His policies were not directly to blame for people dying in foreign fields. No harm, no crime? When his masters decided it was time for him to go, he simply refused. They had placed him there, sponsored him, kept him out of trouble, and he just threw it back in their faces.

Since the dawn of time – in parliamentary terms – politicians have been getting up to all sorts of things and have been protected by the system. This has always been cross-party. They are all at it. They will all protect each other. Yes, the party on the opposite side of the floor to any transgressor may make little noises when something comes to light, but the issues will normally just be allowed to fizzle and die. The theory being that they can rely on unspoken support across the floor when indiscretions are uncovered. The only time that salacious gossip gets into the open and allowed to fester is when their own party is causing the leakages. If the opposition were to do that, it would be an all-out war, and there would be blood on the carpet. As a result of these backroom political shenanigans, Johnson, after he had stuck two fingers up to his paymasters, kept getting all these allegations coming his way. He had been at it for years, and not a peep was heard. All of a sudden, his entire personal life is exposed. This wasn't an accident, and it didn't come from opposition parties. This came from the heart of his party. They could use this stuff to get rid of him easily. The opposition obviously jumped on it, but they were meant to. That is why the stories were leaked.

Bozza's days were now numbered. The Tory party is in disarray. They are unelectable – not that that has ever stopped them – and they need a replacement for him. Someone who is going to be another fall guy. They don't want to put their favoured people in there; they cannot win an election. It will just be a keyholder position until after the next election. No party leader ever survives an election defeat regardless of the circumstances, so this would be entirely temporary. They would need someone who would just be there. Say nothing, do nothing, just turn up to work and occupy the chair and read the cues he/she was supplied with. They would then have to find someone else after the election that would at least be a credible opposition for a while to give them the opportunity to find their next golden boy. Enter Liz Truss. No credibility, no clue, no chance of winning the next election. Her only job is to stay in the chair until the next general election. That didn't work. Just a little too clueless. A little too incredible. Exit Liz Truss fifty days later and enter candidate number two. This is Rishi Sunak. I suppose this is the guy they expected to take over from Truss to form a shadow cabinet while they try to find the next Eton/Oxbridge leader that will do what he is told. He will be thrown to the wolves in due course, but please, please don't screw up quite so spectacularly. At least get us to the next election.

The Labour Party are now going through a settled period. They can see that they will probably win the next election. They have a bland, uncontroversial leader who isn't going to frighten the electorate. It should be a gimme. I find it a pity that this is the way they think. The UK government have not had an effective opposition since the 70s. Jeremy Corbyn seemed to be the man who would do this. Unfortunately, his strength is to be a thorn in the side of leaders; it is not leadership itself. He could not pull his party into a coherent electable unit because that isn't what he does best. So bland it has to be.

Those shadowy figures that hold the balance of power in the Tory Party have a job on their hands. I suspect the people they are looking to are not in the public eye yet. At least I hope not. I look at the party now and see the worst of humanity. I look towards the Labour party and find them frightened of their own shadows. I look towards the LibDems and see acres of nothing whatsoever. It is depressing to think that we have to legitimise someone's political career in the next general election. Some say that we should have Australia's system where everyone is legally required to vote. If they put that in place, we need to insist that the political parties do their bit and advance at least one candidate that is electable. They don't have that yet.

CONCLUSION

End of rant. You, the reader, now have the benefit of knowing my take on the shit-show that is the human race. I, on the other hand have no idea whether you have been spitting feathers and swearing at every syllable or nodding sagely at each opinion and saying, "yes, that sounds about right." As the whole thing is premised on the idea that they are my opinions with a little research, I suspect you'd be, as ever, somewhere between the two extremes. I will close with these thoughts:

Don't believe anything just because you want it to be true. Believe it because it is true.

Don't believe that, if you are of a particular political hue that the other side of the fence is automatically wrong. Some of the nastiest political figures in history got some things right.

Don't believe that because you have dangly bits between your legs, that your opinion is more or less valid than those who don't. it is the substance of the opinion that counts.

Don't believe that because you have a dietary preference, that everyone else's is wrong, they are just different.

The first rule of communication is to listen. If you don't listen to the person with whom you are communicating, then you can't agree or disagree.

Finally, do believe that anything said in a pub is bullshit until proven otherwise, when sober, and nowhere near the pub. Everyone talks bollox in pubs, that is that they are there for.

Made in the USA
Middletown, DE
26 February 2024